MYSTERIES
OF
THE UNIVERSE
AND
RUMI'S DISCOVERIES ON
THE
MAJESTIC PATH OF LOVE

BY

DR. MAJID M. NAINI

Universal Vision & *Research*

MYSTERIES OF THE UNIVERSE AND RUMI'S DISCOVERIES ON THE MAJESTIC PATH OF LOVE. Copyright © 2002 by Dr. Majid M. Naini. All rights reserved. Printed in the United States of America. No part of this book may be reproduced or transmitted in any form or by any means, electronic or mechanical, including photocopying, recording, or by any information storage and retrieval system, without written permission from the author, except for brief quotations embedded in critical articles and reviews about this book.

Published by
Universal Vision and Research
P.O. Box 7401
Delray Beach, Florida 33482
U.S.A.

Email: Rumi@naini.net

Web Site: www.naini.net

Cover Painting by Dr. Fereydoun Parsa

Library of Congress Cataloging-in-Publication Data is available from the publisher.

ISBN 0-9714600-0-0

بنام حضرت عشق

IN THE NAME OF THE SUPREME MASTER
CREATOR OF THE UNIVERSE
THE GOD OF LOVE

MYSTERIES
OF
THE UNIVERSE
AND
RUMI'S DISCOVERIES ON
THE
MAJESTIC PATH OF LOVE

سر خوشان عشق را نالان مکن   ای خدا این وصل را هجران مکن

قصد این مستان و این بستان مکن   باغ جان را تازه و سر سبز دار

خلق را مسکین و سرگردان مکن   چون خزان بر شاخ و برگ دل مزن

هرچ خواهی کن و لیکن آن مکن   نیست در عالم ز هجران تلخ تر

Oh God, please sever not this union,

Let not the ecstatic of love cry.

Keep fresh and green the garden of life,

Ruin not this garden and these drunken ones.

Like autumn, do not fall on the branch and leaves of the heart,

Make not the people destitute and mystified…

In this world nothing is more bitter than separation;

Do whatever You want,

but please sever not.

(Divane Shams, 2020)

تقدیم به عمو داود عزیز و امیر گرامی که بسوی حضرت عشق
سفر کرده‌اند ولی در قلب من همیشه حاضرند.

تقدیم به همه عاشقان و سرمستان عشق حضرت حق.

To my beloved uncle, Amoo Davood, and my dear nephew,
Amir, who have departed from this world and are continuing
their majestic journeys toward the God of Love. They
are forever present in my heart and thoughts.

To all who are intoxicated with God's love.

مرده بدم زنده شدم گریه بدم خنده شدم

دولت عشق آمدومن دولت پاینده شدم

I was dead,

I became alive,

I was tears,

I became laughter;

The majesty of love came,

and I became an everlasting majesty myself.

(Divane Shams, 1393)

هر که اندر عشق یابد زندگی   کفر باشد پیش او جز بندگی

Whoever finds life in love,

Except servitude (to God), all is blasphemy.

(Mathnavi Book 5, Verse 1866)

CONTENTS

INTRODUCTION AND MOTIVATION   1

SECTION I: RUMI'S LIFE AND TRANSFORMATION   7

1. A BRIEF BIOGRAPHY OF RUMI   9

2. THE FATEFUL MEETING WITH SHAMS   19
    Shams' First Disappearance   32
    The Arrival of Shams' Letter   34
    Sending for Shams   39
    The Return of Shams   42
    Shams' Second Disappearance With No Return   45

3. THE MYSTERY OF SHAMS, THE ETERNAL BIRD   49
    Rumi's Unsuccessful Search for Shams   53

4. RUMI'S FIRST KHALIFEH, SALAH-UDDIN ZARKOOB   59

5. RUMI'S TRUE SAMAA   67

6. RUMI'S SECOND KHALIFEH, HOSAM-UDDIN   71
    Composing Mathnavi   74
    Rumi's Exceptional Love for Hosam-uddin   82

7. RUMI'S BIG VENTURE AND GAMBLE ON LOVE   85
    What is Love?   86
    Love and Fear   99

SECTION II: RUMI'S DISCOVERIES ON THE MAJESTIC PATH OF LOVE 109

1. THE UNIVERSE, SCIENCE, TECHNOLOGY, AND REALITY 111
The Creation of the Universe 114
The Creation of Heaven and Earth 116
Why God Created the Universe 118
Everything in the Universe Praises God 120
The Earth's Rotation 124
Nuclear Explosion 126
The Higher Senses 128
The Spectrum of Frequencies 130
Light and Color 135
The True Reality and the Perception of Reality 137
Our Contradictory and Turbulent World and Its Makeup
and the Hegelian Dialectic 140
The Origin of Music and the Reason We Love It 146
The Continual Renewal of Our Bodies and the World 149

2. LIFE JOURNEY AND HUMAN NATURE 153
Human's Journey from Solid to Infinity 154
The Diverse Forms and Stages of the Nature of Man from the Beginning 158
The Nature of Human Beings 162
The Caravan of Life 165

3. DIVINE DESTINY 167
Divine Destiny and Regrets 168
Destined to Make Mistakes 172
Being at Peace with the World 175
Beyond Soil, Water, Wind, Fire, Heaven, and Earth 177
Divine Destiny Cannot Be Escaped 180
Be Careful What You Wish For 182
Our Sustenance or Daily Provisions 183
The Story of Holy Jesus and the Fool 188

4. RELATING TO GOD 191

If You Desire Paradise, Do Not Ask Anything from Anyone 192

The Story of Holy Moses and the Shepherd 193

5. THE HUMAN BODY, MIND, SOUL, POWER, AND ACTIONS 201

The Light of God is Man's Original Food 202

Man's Power 203

Our Inner Dragon 204

Good Deeds Never Die 208

Happiness is a State of Mind and Thoughts 209

Never Give Up 210

Take Control of Your Own Core Center 211

Why People Use Drugs and Alcohol 214

6. FRIENDS AND ENEMIES 215

Spiritual Connection and Attraction 216

Let Us Appreciate One Another 217

Your Enemies Are Your Medicine 219

Your Three Companions in This World 223

7. BE CAREFUL WHO YOU FOLLOW 225

False Assumptions 226

Beware of the Charlatans and Imposters 227

Philosophers Prolong and Complicate Your Path 230

8. REPENTENCE, PRAYER, AND THE DAY OF JUSTICE 233

Repentance 234

Prayer Repels Tragedy 238

The Day Of Justice 240

9. THE MAGIC OF LOVE 243

10. THE TRUE PATH   **255**
    The True Occupation   256
    We Are Nothing Without God's Grace   257

ACKNOWLEDGMENTS   **259**

BOOK COVER PAINTING   **260**
    Excerpts from Dr. Parsa's Letter Explaining the Painting   262
    Dr. Parsa's Letter in Farsi Calligraphy   264

ENDNOTES   **268**

INDEX   **269**

ABOUT THE AUTHOR   **274**

INTRODUCTION AND MOTIVATION

I am delighted that Rumi's poetry is being published more and more in many languages throughout the world. Many of Rumi's poems that have appeared lately in English are interpretations of translations from the original Farsi (Persian language) texts and relate to the subject of love. In addition, there has not been much explanatory background available regarding Rumi's verses. One of my main motives for writing this book has been to reveal new aspects of Rumi's profound discoveries and insights to the reader. In this book I have tried to let Rumi express himself through his own most fascinating and magnificent verses and stories, and to set forth some features of Rumi's road map for reaching the highest states of serenity and ecstasy. Toward this end I have presented my own translations from Rumi's original texts in Farsi, and provided comments about Rumi's transformation and poetry where useful.

I have selected the poems and information from the most accurate sources and incorporated the works of the most respected and renowned Rumi researchers and historians. I believe they are among the best and most authentic works written in both Farsi and English. I have referenced most of the verses in accordance with *Mathnavi*, edited by Dr. Reynold A. Nicholson and *Kulliyate Divane Shams* - Dr. Foroozanfar's edition, printed by Amir Kabir Press. There are a few verses that are found in different versions of *Divane Shams* and *Mathnavi*, but not included in the above editions.

I have tried to keep the integrity and, particularly, the essence of all verses intact by attempting to refrain from projecting my own thoughts and opinions into the translations from Farsi. I have, however, added my own commentary whenever I thought it was necessary. I have endeavored to be as accurate as possible in order to ensure that I have faithfully preserved and presented Rumi's most profound and insightful thoughts and teachings even though this has sometimes resulted in the loss of poetic meter in the translation of the verses. I believe that this precision is essential to learning Rumi's practical methods and teachings, through which human beings can reach inner peace and live joyfully in this turbulent and troublesome world. It is amazing that one who truly follows Rumi's insights and teachings, can not only learn how to live happily in this world, but also peacefully and productively with oneself and others. Rumi actually shows anyone how to appreciate the wonderful journey of life both in time and space on this earth, throughout the universe, and beyond.

Please keep in mind that due to major differences between the Persian and English languages, sometimes it is almost impossible to transfer the magnificent meaning and the quintessence of Rumi's verses into English. Sometimes there are no corresponding words and terms in English but, in my translations, I have done my best to maintain the essence and meaning of Rumi's profound visions and teachings through his revitalizing poems. Unfortunately, another undesirable casualty of any English translation of Rumi's poetry is the loss of the heart-reviving rhythms. Rumi's poetry, in general, is based upon musical rhythms. Since he composed and channeled many verses while he was turning and performing Samaa (whirling dance), the beat can easily be felt underneath his beautiful words. The intimate connection between his poetry and music is vividly portrayed in the story of the day that Rumi was passing through the bazaar and suddenly heard the sound of the hammer striking the anvil from a goldsmith shop. This beat affected him so intensely that he started to turn and dance and spontaneously compose some beautiful *Ghazals* (verses in a special style of poetry) that I will present later. For the above reasons, I have included the original Farsi verses for the benefit of those who are privileged to read and understand Farsi. I hope reading the verses in Farsi will add to their pleasure as Farsi is the language of love, poetry, and rhythm. I also thought this might provide an introduction to the Farsi language and writing style for those who are not yet familiar with Farsi.

Rumi's poetry sometimes appears deceptively simple, but it is actually very complex if one understands the deeper meanings of his verses and his usage of words and rhythms. Rumi's works are so profound that one can study them for many years, from several different perspectives, yet still find that some of his verses remain elusive. Through my own experience, although it may be hard to believe, it has taken me close to twenty years to understand certain lines of Rumi's poetry during times of meditation and higher spiritual awareness and consciousness. The following is a good example:

(Mathnavi Book 3, starting from Verse 463)

کز جهان زنده ز اول آمدیم
باز از پستی سوی بالا شدیم

جمله اجزا در تحرک در سکون
ناطقان کانا الیه راجعون

ذکر و تسبیحات اجزای نهان
غلغلی افکند اندر آسمان

We have come at first from a living world,
Again from this low end we soar to that high end (world).
All the particles in motion or motionless,
Are stating, "Verily we all return to God."
The chanting and the praises of hidden particles,
Have put such an uproar in the sky.

For the past thirty years of my life, I have been blessed and privileged to have had Rumi by my side as my spiritual teacher and guide, throughout the four continents (Africa, Asia, Europe, and America) on which I have lived, studied, and taught. During the most discouraging times of my life, Rumi's insight, wisdom, profound teachings, and astoundingly beautiful verses have reminded me of the Supreme Creator's love and mercy and have kept my faith strong, my vision clear, and my morale high. Rumi has encouraged me to hold my head high and keep my integrity intact. He has helped me to continue my journey of life on the majestic path of love and discovery during many tumultuous times.

3

I have had the honor of being in the presence of highly enlightened and spiritually evolved scholars. I have learned a wealth of knowledge from these learned individuals, especially in relation to Rumi, and I am very much indebted to them. My formal academic education, training, and professional life have been in the areas of electronics engineering and computer and information science and technology. This scientific and technical background has also helped me tremendously in understanding Rumi's insights and discoveries through the eye of science and technology. I have often been amazed that around 750 years ago, Rumi vividly and clearly explained in his verses about the force of gravity, quantum physics, the world of frequencies, nuclear physics, dialectic philosophy, astronomy, and many other fascinating scientific facts and subjects.

Through all the works and writings that I have had the fortune of reading, hearing, and analyzing, I have never come across any work that looks at Rumi's poetry and storytelling from the perspective of science and technology. I hope this new angle will add to the joy and pleasure of those who love Rumi's thoughts and visions as we take one step further in the appreciation of his ingeniousness. In this book I have discussed not only Rumi's guidance for life, but also some of the most important subjects and issues found in Rumi's teachings, especially the ones related to science, technology, and the human condition. Of course, I have also focused on Rumi's emphasis on love with all of its magnificence and splendor. After all, love is the magical force that can quicken the flow of the energy of one's soul and allow one to soar to the highest state of ecstasy so incredibly fast that the concept cannot even fit in one's wildest imagination. When Rumi took his unbelievable venture and gamble on love, he took the path that he realized was the most expeditious. It is no wonder that Rumi according to Aflaaki exclaimed,

"Ghazzali (famous Sufi and theologian) was one of the most learned people in the world,
but if he had a drop of love instead

4

he would have been better off,
because love is the best teacher."

For most of the past twenty-four years I have worked in academia as a Professor, Department Chair, and College Dean in various universities throughout the world in scientific and technical fields. Due to my love for Rumi's visions and teachings expressed through his most meaningful poetry, I have endeavored to write this book not as an academician or in a style that would be geared toward academia. Instead, this book has been written in a simple manner and language in order to share some of my learning with all who love Rumi and admire the majestic path of love that he prescribed and practiced. My intention was to combine all the references and research without burdening the readers with cumbersome details, references, and footnotes. I have summarized all of the most historically accurate references that I have found and merged them to shed light on Rumi's life and his spiritual transformation. In writing Rumi's biography and poetry, I have utilized the works of Dr. Abdul Hussein Zarinkoob, Dr. Foroozanfar, Dr. Abdul Kareem Soroush, Ostad Mohammed Taghi Jafari, Dr. Shafiee Kad Kani, Aflaaki, Jaami, Dr. Reynold A. Nicholson, Afzal Iqbal, Dr. Annemarie Schimmel, and others.[1] For the sake of accuracy, the dates relating to the historical events mentioned in this book are written in accordance with the historical references in the Hejri Ghamari (HG, Islamic lunar calendar), which starts from the Prophet Mohammad's migration from Mecca to Medina in accordance with the lunar calendar. I have tried to provide the approximate equivalents of those dates (HG) in the Gregorian (Western) calendar as well.

5

SECTION I:

RUMI'S LIFE

AND

TRANSFORMATION

8

CHAPTER 1

A BRIEF BIOGRAPHY

OF

RUMI

Molana Jalal-uddin Mohammad Ebne Mohammad Ebne Hussein Balkhy, known as Rumi, the great Sufi (Islamic mystic) poet and mystic lover, was born on September 30, 1207 (Rabial-avval 6; 604 HG) in the city of Balkh, in the Khorasan province of the Persian Empire. Today, Balkh is in Afghanistan, located near Mazar-e Sharif. Rumi left this world on December 7, 1273 (672 HG) in Konya, which is in present-day Turkey. During Rumi's time in Konya, Farsi (Persian language) was the common language used by the court and government systems, as well as scientists, writers, poets, and other learned people. All of Rumi's works are in Farsi, with the exception of some Arabic verses referring to the holy Koran (Islamic holy book) or the Hadith (statements from the holy Prophet Mohammad, peace and blessings be upon him).

Rumi's father, Baha-e-Valad, was a religious scholar, teacher, and preacher who was respected and admired by many people. He also had a keen interest in Sufism (Islamic mysticism) and preferred the Sufi way of practicing and teaching religion (Islam). He would travel to different cities around Balkh to give speeches that were widely attended by many people from all different walks of life. On account of his wisdom and knowledge, he was given the name *Sultan-al-Olama* (King of the Learned Ones). Rumi was a special child who prayed and fasted at a very young age. He was observed weeping while he was praying at the tender age of five. Additional evidence of his uniqueness occurred one day when Rumi was playing with other children on the roof of his house. Someone suggested jumping from his roof to the neighbor's roof. Rumi told them, "Jumping from one roof to another roof is worthy of the dogs and cats, let us fly to the sky." It is stated by Jaami that Rumi unexpectedly disappeared in front of the other children. The children became frightened and screamed. Suddenly, Rumi reappeared with a pale face and bewildered eyes. He told his playmates that a group of people who were wearing green shawls and robes took him to the sky for a tour and then brought him back again.

Rumi's father assigned one of his closet disciples, Seyyed Borhan-uddin Termezi, to be Rumi's teacher. Seyyed Borhan-uddin Termezi taught Rumi the foundations and basics of religion and philosophy at a very early age. Around one year before the Mongolian attack in 1219 (616 HG), when Rumi was about twelve years old, his father left Balkh along with his family, close friends, and followers. At that time, Balkh was under the corrupt reign of Sultan Mohammad Khorazm Shah. It has been stated that Rumi's father's drive for justice and fairness and his frequent speaking out against corruption and injustice aroused animosity toward him among the ruler, power brokers, and other influential people in Balkh.

There were around 300 people traveling in Rumi's caravan from Balkh. On their way to Mecca for the pilgrimage, they first visited the city of Neyshaboor, the birthplace of Omar Khayyam and Attar, the renowned Persian poets and Sufi. In Neyshaboor, Attar came to visit them and presented a handwritten copy of his book entitled *Asrar Nameh* (The Book of Secrets) to Rumi. When Attar saw the young Rumi, he looked at the sky and sighed, stating, "Soon this boy will set fire to the lovers of this world."

Rumi's caravan continued its journey toward Ray and Hamedan (cities in Iran), and then to Baghdad, where they stayed in a school. Baghdad was crowded with refugees fleeing the Mongolian invasion and there were shortages of food and housing. From Baghdad they went to Mecca for Hajj (pilgrimage). From Mecca they traveled to Shaam (today's Syria) and then departed for Larandeh, which was a part of Asia Minor and was called Eastern Rome (part of the former Roman Empire). Today, Larandeh is called Gharaman and is a part of Turkey. During this long journey, they passed through beautiful landscapes, including mountains, valleys, and deserts. The air was filled with the intoxicating fragrance of wild flowers and the mellifluous sounds of caravan music and the singing of wild birds. They beheld spectacular sunrises and sunsets. At night, they slept under a sky bursting with stars. This journey through such magnificent natural beauty had an everlasting impact on the young Rumi, enhancing his imagination, tender feelings, powerful visions, and thoughts.

When they reached Larandeh, Rumi was about eighteen years old. The governor of Larandeh welcomed the family to his territory, which was under Ala-uddin Keighobad Saljooghi's rule. The governor named a school after Rumi's father and gave the family a comfortable place to stay. Larandeh was a captivating, verdant city, filled with gardens and historical structures and sites dating from the ancient Greek and Roman empires. In Larandeh, Rumi's father started teaching in his school. Shortly after their arrival, Rumi's loving mother, Bibi Alavi, passed away to the higher world. Later that year, Rumi married Gohar Khatoon (Lady Jewel), whose father was Khajeh Sharaf-uddin Samarghandi and was from Khorasan, the same region as Rumi and his family. During their four-year stay in Larandeh, God gave Rumi and his wife two sons, who were named Baha-uddin and Ala-uddin.

The ruler of that region, Ala-uddin Kighobad, the first of the Saljooghi dynasty, heard about Rumi's father's fame and knowledge and invited him to Konya, the center of his region. At that time, Konya was also one of the preeminent centers of knowledge and culture, like Balkh and Neyshaboor. Subsequently, Rumi's father and all of his family left Larandeh and went to Konya (1228; 626 HG). Rumi was now twenty-two years old. The family's arrival in Konya was heralded with much fanfare. They were warmly and enthusiastically welcomed by a great number of people from all walks of life who had traveled from a long distance, expressly for the purpose of greeting Rumi's father and his entourage. The Sultan himself welcomed and embraced Rumi's father. It has even been stated that the Sultan kissed his hand as a sign of respect. The Sultan threw a lavish party and invited the town's learned citizens and dignitaries to meet and pay respect to Rumi's father. Many privileged people who were close to the Sultan and his court were interested in this scholarly and knowledgeable man. One of the people from the Sultan's court built a school for Rumi's father, which, after his passing, became Rumi's place of teaching and preaching.

Rumi continued his education in theology, philosophy, literature, poetry, languages, and history. He became so learned that his father allowed him to give lectures in his school. Rumi's lectures were very exciting, informative, and appealing, as he incorporated beautiful stories and Persian poetry to convey his messages and teachings. Soon after his first lecture, Rumi became very popular and his talks were always well attended. As his father grew older and his voice began to weaken, Rumi's sessions became increasingly passionate and exhilarating. The more often his mesmerizing speeches were heard, the more people attended his sessions. As time passed, Rumi gradually took over the religious and teaching duties of his father, and it became natural for the people to see him sit in his father's place of teaching and lecturing.

After two years in Konya, his father passed away at the age of eighty-three years (1231; 628 HG). Rumi was only twenty-four years old at this time. The people of Konya held a grand funeral ceremony for his father and many people from different groups attended the service. The Sultan himself announced one week of official mourning. After his father's passing, Rumi also became responsible for the family in addition to teaching and guiding the students and followers. One year after his father's passing (1232; 629 HG), Seyyed Borhan-uddin Termezi, his childhood teacher and his father's loyal disciple, came to Konya. At this time he was also known as Borhan-uddin Mohaghegh.

Termezi had searched for Rumi's family for a long time after they left their home in Balkh. Upon seeing Termezi, Rumi was reconnected again to his father's world and his origins, in addition to all the beautiful memories of his childhood. Particularly after his father's death, on those days of sadness and longing for his home, seeing Termezi was both a great relief and a wonderful joy. In Termezi's voice, Rumi could hear the voices from his happy childhood and relive the wonderful memories of his father's house in his homeland. Termezi was a dignified elder scholar, learned researcher, and eloquent speaker. He was over sixty years old and he had gained tremendous insight and knowledge through his experiences and association with diversely educated and enlightened people during his travels throughout various places on the way from Balkh to Konya. He loved Rumi's father, his teacher, so much that he considered him superior to all other scholarly and knowledgeable people, except the holy prophets. He loved Rumi like a son and memories of Rumi's father made this love even stronger. His reappearance was a wonderful blessing for Rumi, for it seemed as if his father had returned.

Rumi was not comfortable when the students and followers called him *Molana* (leader and guide), as they used to call his father Molana. Rumi did not believe that he was worthy of that title and felt that he was still far from reaching his father's knowledge and stature. Therefore, Rumi was delighted that once again he had a teacher and guide. Under Termezi's guidance, Rumi continued his learning and spiritual discipline, refinement, and growth. During that period, Rumi spent a lot of time practicing *Cheleh*. Cheleh is a special spiritual retreat lasting forty days when one performs meditations, fasting, and prayers in order to achieve a higher spiritual status.

At the age of twenty-six (1233; 630 HG), with Termezi's encouragement, Rumi left his wife and children and departed for Syria to continue his education. The people of Konya, due to their love and respect for Rumi, ensured that his family would live comfortably and all their needs would be met. In Rumi's absence, Termezi was responsible for the care and educational needs of his young sons. Rumi visited his family during the holidays, caring for his family and household affairs, and monitoring his children's maturation and education. During his visits he saw Termezi and also took advantage of his guidance. Once in a while, Termezi gave a lecture at Rumi's request in his father's school. Termezi's voice and preaching style resembled that of his teacher, Rumi's father. Whenever he lectured, the memories of Rumi's father became alive again. Despite the persistent requests of the followers of Rumi's father and Rumi himself, Termezi purposefully spent the majority of his time during Rumi's absence in a nearby city called Gheysariyeh, a beautiful quiet town and one of the centers of commerce and wealth in that territory (the former Eastern Roman Empire). Apparently, Termezi did not want to remind people of the former exciting sessions held by Rumi's father and entice them to become his own followers. His intention was only to promote the young Molana (Rumi) and replace his father's memory and position with no one except Rumi himself. From this selfless act, one can easily deduce that he genuinely loved Rumi and realized the young man's tremendous potential, thus foreseeing the glorious future awaiting Rumi in the coming years. During the seven years that Rumi was studying outside Konya, Termezi traveled constantly to Konya to look after Rumi's sons and family affairs. He also reminded the followers of Rumi's father about the young Rumi to ensure their continued loyalty.

In Syria, Rumi joined the teaching schools of the Hanafi (an Islamic sect) theologians. He first studied in the city of Halab under Kamal-uddin Ebne Ala-uddin, a well-known theologian in Halab. He came from a tribe of learned theologians and was a *Mufti* (religious authority), one who has reached the stature by which he was entitled to deliver religious decrees (*Fatwas*). He was also very fond of poetry, literature, and history. In order to benefit from the teachings of other scholars and Sufis, Rumi used to travel to Damascus once in a while to spend some time studying in one of the city's prominent schools. It has been said that he met Ebne Arabi (died 1240; 638 HG), the well-known philosopher, during this time in Damascus. In both cities, Rumi studied diligently with the foremost scholars and teachers in all aspects of religion, theology, philosophy, and literature. He used to become so occupied with his studies that at times he neglected to eat and sleep. As a result, he became ill several times from exhaustion. During that time, Rumi also consistently followed Termezi's instructions for meditation, fasting, and chanting (*Zekr*). For part of the year, particularly during the five months of Haraam, it was his custom to fast from dawn until sunset and at night stay up until dawn to chant and read the Koran. Chanting "*Allah*" (God) was his constant mantra. He had learned this from both his father and Termezi. His lengthy prayers were intermingled with tears and supplications. Following this path,

Rumi traveled from the theology of religion to the theology of God (Allah). During his seven years (1232-1239; 630-637 HG) of studying, purification, and contemplation, he was transformed into both a learned theologian and a unitarian *Salek* (a traveler on the journey of discovery on the majestic path of love).

At the age of thirty-three, after seven years in Syria, Rumi returned to Konya. At that time he was considered to be the greatest theologian of his time. There was a rumor that the new Sultan, Ghiyas-uddin Keykhosro, wrote to Rumi's teachers at the beginning of his reign and requested that Rumi honor them with his return to Konya. Upon Rumi's arrival, the dignitaries, scholars, people of high stature, and individuals from all different classes of society came to welcome him back to Konya. When Termezi met with Rumi, he was delighted to discover that Rumi met all of his high expectations. He felt extremely proud of his former student, since he was aware that the son of his beloved teacher had indeed become a great scholar and *Sheikh* (spiritual guide and teacher) like his blessed father, superior to all others in his own time and region. Unfortunately, this was the last meeting between them, as at the age of seventy-eight, Termezi passed from this world shortly after his return to Gheysariyeh (1240; 638 HG). When Rumi was informed about Termezi's death, he immediately went to Gheysariyeh and arranged a funeral worthy of his beloved teacher. Since Termezi had no heirs, Rumi donated and distributed whatever Termezi had left to the poor and underprivileged people. With the loss of his old teacher and spiritual guide, once again sadness and sorrow returned to Rumi's life. His grief was further intensified, as Termezi's death became as a reminder of his father's death. Rumi would never forget Termezi's teachings and statements. One of Termezi's greatest sayings was, "Knowing God becomes complete when forgetting everybody else becomes possible." Another one of his great sayings was, "Escaping from everything is easy - escaping from *Nafs* (sensual desires or carnal soul) is difficult and Nafs is the root of all evils."

After Termezi's death, Rumi mainly preferred to stay alone. However, he continued teaching, preaching, praying, educating and raising his children, and taking care of his family affairs. When his older son, Baha-uddin, known as Sultan-Valad, reached the age of seventeen (1241; 639 HG), he began appearing with his father in public and seemed like Rumi's younger brother. His younger son, Ala-uddin, who was around fifteen years old, was also loved by his caring father. Rumi sent both sons to Syria to continue their education, even though the separation was both difficult for their mother and Rumi. The two brothers were not very close, and the distance was a source of concern for their mother. Once in a while, Rumi and his wife would hear news of conflict between the brothers and learned that they were not making great progress in their studies. Rumi wrote letters to each son, attempting to establish peace and friendship between them and emphasizing the importance of being conscientious students and considerate of their household workers.

To distract himself from missing his children and his wife's concerns, Rumi became more focused on his work. Outside of his house, his time was dedicated to teaching, preaching, guiding, and giving Fatwas (religious decrees). Knowledge-seekers from everywhere rushed to him and his many loving followers added to the enthusiasm and excitement of his lectures. His older son Sultan-Valad stated that sometimes over 10,000 students and followers would gather to listen to their beloved Sheikh and teacher. At the request of other famous schools in Konya, Rumi taught in their establishments as well as his own. He was also constantly invited to the houses of his followers, the Sufi *Khaneghah* (Sufi temple), and gatherings of *Akhiyan* (brothers), a group well known for their righteousness and good deeds. In all those sessions Rumi, with his amazing story-telling talent and lyrical tendencies, incorporated a great deal of beautiful poetry (not his own) into his lectures and teachings. His unique style energized those sessions to such a degree that gradually, other lecturers' sessions became empty, leading to anger and jealousy on the part of his competitors. Rumi's expertise in the Koran, Hadith (the Prophet Mohammad's statements), poetry, and folklore parables mesmerized his listeners and audiences. His answers to their questions were full of profound and intricate points that they had not heard before. Even those who had experienced the pleasure of attending his father's sessions now found that the young Rumi's sessions were even warmer and more stimulating. Samples of those sessions can be found in a collection called *Majalese-Sab-eh* (Seven Sessions). In those lectures, as is apparent from the samples, Rumi speaks about the Koran, Hadith, prayers, and talking to God. Intermingled with the stories of the prophets and great righteous men, his lectures were interspersed with lovely Persian poetry, full of fables and teaching symbols.

Many of Rumi's followers accompanied him on his travels back and forth. When he passed through neighborhoods and alleys with his large entourage it was difficult for other pedestrians to move around. The people who accompanied him ranged from the young, such as Hosam-uddin Chalapi, to the elders such as Salah-uddin, a goldsmith in Konya. Only a short time after his return to Konya, Rumi had become exceptionally popular and loved by the overwhelming majority of the people from all classes of society. As he passed through the streets of Konya, people often requested religious Fatwas (religious decrees) and requested help if they had any problems or had been oppressed by powerful people. It was well known in the region that Rumi's mediation with rulers and influential people was well received and usually very effective. Everybody considered him to be the greatest theologian, scholar, and religious leader of the region, the grand Sheikh. Other theologians were envious of his fame and status.

After the death of his wife, Gohar Khatoon (1242; 640 HG), Rumi married a widow named Kera Khatoon. His second wife had two children from her previous marriage, a boy and a girl whose name was Keymia Khatoon.

18

CHAPTER 2

THE FATEFUL MEETING

WITH

SHAMS

زاهد کشوری بودم صاحب منبری بدم
کرد قضا دل مرا عاشق و کف زنان تو

I was the devout of a country,
I owned a pulpit,
Divine Destiny forced my heart
to love you and clap for you.

(Divane Shams, 2152)

On a fateful Saturday (November 29, 1245; 642 HG) at the age of thirty-eight, Rumi was returning home after his daily work at his school. He was riding on a beautiful horse through the bazaar, his entourage of young and old students and followers accompanying him, when a stranger suddenly pushed aside the crowd, grabbed his horse's reins, and stopped him. This stranger, whose name was Shams, appeared to be a vagabond over the age of sixty. He stared into Rumi's eyes and asked him in a loud voice that echoed under the bazaar's high ceiling, *"Was the Prophet Mohammad, peace and blessings be upon him, higher, or Bayazid?"* Rumi, in an angry and aggressive voice, responded, *"The Prophet Mohammad, peace and blessings be upon him, was the top link of the prophets. How can Bayazid be at the same level as him?"* Then Shams replied, *"Then why is it that the Prophet stated, 'Praise and glory to Thee (God) that we have not recognized Thee as it behooves,' and Bayazid stated, 'Praise and glory to me, for how grand is my stature?'"* Rumi paused for a moment and responded that Bayazid (the renowned Sufi Sheikh) was impatient and with one sip of God's love was making a loud drunken uproar, but the Prophet had the capacity of an ocean and did not lose his calm and wisdom even with a whole jug of God's love. It was a fascinating question and answer. Rumi became silent for a moment and looked at the stranger's eyes. In that quick gaze between the two of them, their strangeness was transformed into familiarity. That short glance created a deep connection between their hearts and souls. Some sources have even reported that Rumi fainted upon hearing that question, realizing that neither the man nor the question was ordinary.

In any event, their hearts and souls told each other whatever there was to be said. Shams' look must have told Rumi, "I have come searching for you from a long distance, but with this heavy load of knowledge, thoughts, and stature how can you arrive at God's meeting?" Rumi's look must have responded, "Oh dervish, do not leave me; stay with me and let me be free of this heavy load which is tiring my shoulders and my whole existence." Rumi became intoxicated from this question and Shams also, as he later stated, became euphoric from Rumi's intoxication. This dialogue between the two scholars had an incredible effect on both of them. Under the gaze of that strange dervish, Rumi felt like a defenseless pigeon under the shadow of a bald eagle. No one had ever asked Rumi such a deep and meaningful question, which put religion face to face with mysticism. Rumi's heavy and cold arrogance melted under the warmth of the stranger's look and was replaced with feelings of gratitude and humility. He yielded to this strange champion who had taken him down from his high horse of pride and status. He descended from his horse, both literally and figuratively, and started walking toward his home shoulder to shoulder with the stranger. Then, Rumi invited the mysterious guest to his house, hoping to be liberated from the chains of dependencies that had been shackling his hands, feet and whole being.

There are other stories that are not well documented historically about that fateful meeting between Rumi and that mysterious stranger Shams. One such story relates that one day Shams entered Rumi's teaching session and interrupted him. Shams pointed to some of the books in front of Rumi and asked him, "What are these?" Rumi responded pompously, "This is something that you would not know." Suddenly the books caught on fire. Rumi was astonished and asked Shams, "What is going on?" This time Shams answered Rumi in a similar manner, "This is something that you wouldn't know." As the story goes, when Shams left, Rumi followed him and left everything behind.

Another story recounts that Shams entered Rumi's teaching session, when he and his students were sitting around a little pool of water. Shams asked Rumi about the books spread around him. Rumi responded, "These are the books of knowledge and what are they to you?" Shams then took the books and threw them one by one into the pool. When Rumi angrily objected to this action, Shams ordered the books to return from the pool to their original position without being wet or damaged. Rumi, bewildered by this action, asked him the secret of that deed. He responded, "This is from jubilation and ecstasy and what is it to you?"

There is also another story that one day Shams entered Rumi's school pretending to be a seller of halva (sweets). Rumi bought some halva, ate it, suddenly became insane, left the school, ran after the man, and did not return to the school. However, as I mentioned earlier, there are doubts about the historical authenticity of these anecdotes. What is certain is that this sudden and unbelievable meeting must have taken Rumi back to the spiritual visions and discoveries of his boyhood, especially that time on the rooftop of his house in Balkh. At the time of his momentous meeting with Shams, Rumi must have traveled from the world of theology and philosophy, a physical and earthly reality, to a higher spiritual and mysterious realm. For Rumi, this journey must have been reminiscent of the teachings of his beloved father and his teacher, Termezi, who had taught him the difference between the knowledge of philosophy and the knowledge of spirituality. In fact, Termezi had instructed him to combine the knowledge of spirituality with the knowledge of philosophy and theology. The question that Shams had asked Rumi about the Prophet Mohammad and Bayazid was not about the inward knowledge (*Elme Hal*) and the outward knowledge (*Elme Ghal*), but concerned with the experience of the heart.

Meeting the stranger Shams helped Rumi to gain the courage to cut all the chains and remove the veils that had been suffocating him. This brief conversation taught him that in order to attain his freedom, he had to first find the courage to abandon his position, fame, books, lessons, and schools. It also reminded him of the childhood experience of his own soaring power that seemed to have left him during his long years of schooling and studying. This predestined meeting, which on the surface seemed like an accident, was the beginning of Rumi's metamorphosis. Amazingly Rumi, an official theologian and the religious authority of the region, had instantaneously been transformed into a dervish (mystic) poet who had fallen hopelessly in love with the Supreme Master Creator of the Universe, the God of Love.

Seclusion with Shams was the beginning of Rumi's new existence. This was not a scientific or intellectual retreat. Instead, it was a spiritual seclusion. Due to the companionship and guidance of the strange old man, and their conversations, Rumi was able to free himself from all the obstacles that were preventing him from soaring to the heights of his potential on his journey of discovery on the majestic path of love toward the Divine.

From the first day of their meeting, Rumi and Shams left Rumi's house and school and went to the house of Salah-uddin, who had become fond of Shams at their very first encounter. Salah-uddin was honored that the privilege of looking after their needs in his own house had been bestowed upon him. Rumi's family, who knew of his whereabouts, rarely received permission to come and visit. However, his eldest son, Baha-uddin, was allowed to visit Salah-uddin's house. Rumi, who was accustomed to reading regularly, abandoned his books in preference to listening and talking to Shams. During their seclusion of three or more months, there was actually no time for any reading. In the presence of Shams, Rumi had entered into a new world, one far removed from his students, followers, and former life. When Rumi was listening to Shams, he could envision a magnificent distant world, a place that he had never experienced during all of his years of studying, preaching, and teaching.

Although Rumi's older son (who was around twenty years old at that time) was fond of their guest, his younger son, who was heavily involved in school and books as Rumi had been at a younger age, was suspicious of this strange old man who had alienated his father from everybody. Rumi's wife harbored the same negative feelings toward Shams. Rumi's students and followers were also discontented. In his isolation, not only had Rumi forgotten about his teachings, but also their well known Sheikh, teacher, and guide had become like a school child in front of the strange old man. They were also very angry that Rumi's separation had denied them the pleasure of being with Rumi and continuing their education and learning.

During that time, however, Rumi had lost himself in Shams and was oblivious to everything else. He seemed to fall deeper in love and become more connected with Shams as their association continued. With every day that passed, he felt that his love for this little old man had increased. Rumi's love for Shams was greater than his love for anyone else. He loved Shams' frank and straightforward talk and the fact that under Shams' power and influence, he was becoming a new person. For Shams' sake he forgot everything, including his lectures, lessons, fame, and high rank. He even forgot about the respect and admiration he had received in his school, home, and the entire region. Without any reservations, Rumi found himself following Shams like a shadow. To be in Shams' presence, Rumi was ready to leave everything and everyone behind and become a vagabond, wandering from city to city and street to street.

Shams had become a window to the hidden world of Allah (God), connecting Rumi to this mystical, unseen place and hence becoming Rumi's whole world. Rumi had found a new love in Shams that he adored with every fiber of his being. This new reality and love had no boundaries and was infinite. During this time, Shams' companionship made any other friendship superfluous. For Rumi, Shams was a superior being, above any other human being he had met and beyond the limited physical world. Until then, Rumi had not seen an individual with such grandeur. When Rumi looked at Shams, he could actually view the invisible world since, in the reflection of the light of his eyes, Rumi could see a ray of God's light. Later Rumi explained this clearly in some of his verses in *Mathnavi*:

(Mathnavi, Mohammad T. Marefat Edition, Book 1, Page 4)

آفتاب است و ز انوار حق است شمس تبریزی که نور مطلق است

Shams of Tabriz who is pure light,
He is a sun and from God's lights,

In those days of solitude with Shams, Rumi was transformed into a humble student, revisiting the memories of his

24

spiritual visions during his childhood in Khorasan. The emotion that he experienced could not be articulated, but he could feel the infinite love and its grand spiritual glory. It seemed as if he were being dissolved within an infinite being and existence. This love was not an ordinary feeling of affection and pleasure like that experienced by ordinary people through sexual and other worldly desires. It was beyond loss and profit; it was unique and exceptional, beyond any usual experience, seeking only perfection and connecting him to a world beyond anyone's imagination. In this love, the lover and beloved had united and become one. This love would take both of them to an identity beyond their limited selves. This love was a blazing fire that burned Rumi's intellect and perception with the shining light of a new revelation. It separated him from himself and melted him in an everlasting existence. This love was beyond intellect, traditions, and all thoughts of self-interest. This newfound love was above praying. In his privacy with Shams, Rumi found intimacy with God. During this time of seclusion and long conversations free of others, Shams uprooted Rumi's old world and existence. Shams had taken him to his own reality and world, which was the world of exultation, jubilation, and pure love.

No one knew anything about Shams, this stranger who was over sixty years old and had spent his lifetime anonymously seeking and traveling. His life was unsettled and unpredictable. Shams, whose father was Ali Ebne Malekdaad Tabrizi, had been a schoolteacher who moved from one city to another and opened schools for children, but since his teaching style and expectations were very strict and demanding, children did not remain in his schools for long and he moved on to the next place. Shams had met most of the scholars, Sufis (Islamic mystics), and other spiritual and eminently knowledgeable people of his own time, and had found them to be too busy with themselves, other people, and the physical world. He had consistently run away from those arrogant prominent people. Many times he had even scolded those individuals, telling them that they were preventing themselves from comprehending the truth. He had traveled from Tabriz to Konya, passing through many cities, staying for a

25

while and then moving on. He had spent most of his life on long journeys and had seen many theologians, philosophers, and learned scholars. However, it was only in Konya that he had found a man who truly understood him and recognized his essence and tenderness. Before Rumi, no one had resonated with his spiritual wavelength and discovered his true spirit.

In fact, Shams' one aspiration in life was to free the knowledge-seekers from themselves so they could concentrate only on God. Shams was asking Rumi to remove what his intellect had put in front of the heart. He was also beseeching Rumi to sacrifice his fame, status, wealth, respect, and acceptance for the glory of God's love. Shams was actually endeavoring to liberate Rumi from the prison of self and dependencies, which had chained his magnificent potential. He was tearing away the fabric of his scholarly arrogance and grandeur. He was attempting to free himself from the veil of his own thoughts and intellect. In those days, if he asked Rumi for his sake to go to a neighborhood and buy a carafe of wine, carry it around his neck, and bring it to him, Rumi would not find this request difficult and would immediately obey. Rumi knew that this kind of request was designed to break his pompous pride and release him from the entrapment of fame and selfishness, which was in reality nothing more than imprisonment and confinement. His brave willingness to obey Shams' instructions indicated his deep commitment in the struggle with the self. He realized that one couldn't set foot on the majestic path of love and journey of discovery without this conflict.

Shams had forbidden Rumi from reading and deliberating on any books. Instead of practicing righteous hardship, he instructed him to do Samaa (whirling dance). According to Shams' belief, there was no better way for the men of God to disconnect from the world of desires and dependencies. He believed that through music and Samaa a human could connect to the higher spiritual world, a world full of aspiration and divine ecstasy. In following Shams, Rumi separated himself from his school, students, and followers. Teaching, preaching, school, and lessons held no attraction for him anymore. Lecturing and

26

instructing people were now seen only as boasting and self-promotion to him. Shams even directed him not to read two of his favorite books, *Favayed Valad* (Rumi's father's book) and *Divane Motonab-bee* (Motonab-bee's book of poetry), which he used to read before and during his studying in Syria. Shams took those books from him and told him that they were like veils that conceal the human essence under their superficial cover and imprison a person within the traps of intellect.

In their spiritual retreat, Rumi was immersed in the stunning and magical sound of the reed, the enchanting music, and Samaa that carried him to an incredible state of ecstasy and delight. Shams communicated with him in statements that were brief, but full of meaning. Whatever was not possible to express with words, Shams would communicate with his eyes and through the language of Samaa. Shams told Rumi profound stories and parables, using examples from the grand Sheikhs and teachers of the past. During those long hours of spiritual seclusion, Rumi reveled in listening to Shams' voice. When Shams was quiet, Rumi could hear the language of silence, music, and Samaa, which was like the language of heaven. Gradually everything disappeared in Shams' voice, look, and euphoric state. For Rumi, everything, including himself, was vanishing. He felt as if he were being consumed in the flame of love. Whatever was in the world at that moment was transformed into Shams. Even the sunlight coming through the window was becoming Shams. The air in his lungs, which caused life and happiness, became Shams' breath. The doors and walls of the house were Shams. The grand sky was Shams. Beyond the skies was Shams. Even the love created in his heart by chanting "Allah" reminded him of Shams.

After about three months, Rumi emerged from his spiritual retreat. He no longer bore any resemblance to the Rumi that had existed prior to meeting Shams. After that fateful day, no one ever saw Rumi riding his horse with that celebrated dignity and pride, surrounded by his admiring entourage. The storytellers in the city spread rumors that the grand Sheikh had lost his mind. They alleged that a stranger in the attire of a halva seller had given Rumi a piece of halva that stole his intellect and sanity, forcing him to follow that halva seller and never return to his school. Rumi was not bothered by these rumors. After this long spiritual seclusion, he looked at everything differently. He had more compassion and love for everyone. The pride and overconfidence, which always seem to be especially evident in eminent scholars and theologians, had completely disappeared in him. Rumi no longer saw anyone as a stranger. He would not humiliate, insult, or condemn anyone. He perceived those around him as images of a smaller world that mirrored the larger world. This rebirth had indeed transformed an ordinary man, who was dependent on eating and sleeping like any other man, into a godly man who had moved beyond the realm of the ordinary.

When Rumi returned amongst his followers, everyone was still fond of him, but he was only fond of Shams. Shams had become his guide and mentor, as Termezi had been during his youth. It seemed that, in his rebirth, Rumi needed a spiritual mentor again, and Shams was an ideal one. Despite the fact that the isolation period was over, Rumi still spent most of his time with Shams. He canceled his preaching and teaching sessions. His followers could only have the pleasure of seeing Rumi during Samaa gatherings, which consisted mainly of the dance and did not allow much time for conversations. In the city, the people considered Samaa an unacceptable new phenomenon, one that angered Rumi's followers and students. Instead of his own lectures, Rumi arranged sessions in which Shams spoke and Rumi, like his own disciples, was a silent listener. The report of those meetings is found in *Maghalote Shams* (Shams' Essays). Those discourses were written based upon Rumi's instructions to his followers.

Shams' manner of speech was harsh, frank, and often stinging. Rumi's students, who were accustomed to Rumi's warm and kind manner of speaking, did not appreciate Shams' offensive style and remarks. They started complaining and expressing their dissatisfaction. Some even objected, asking, "Who is this Shams that somebody like Rumi has become his follower?" They were particularly distressed when they saw

Rumi, with all of his knowledge and intellect, sitting like a child in front of his father when he was with this old drifter from Tabriz. Rumi's unusual behavior was certainly a source of disappointment and shame for them. They even became more annoyed when the news of an incident, indicating Rumi's strong respect for Shams, spread around the town. One day, Jalal-uddin Gharatay, the famous ruler of Konya, arranged a celebration to mark the completion of a large school construction. Everyone in the town and the surrounding area was invited. Prominent citizens, scholars, theologians, Sufis, Akhiyans, and other groups were included and there was a discussion among the scholars and learned people about the most prestigious place to sit in that gathering. Everybody stated his view. Rumi emphatically stated, "The high place is near your beloved." He then arose from his place among the important scholars and went to the side where the ordinary people without name or fame were sitting and sat right next to Shams. This action was considered insulting toward the distinguished guests, while showing great admiration for Shams.

Shams commanded Rumi's supporters in the same manner that he ordered Rumi himself. Rumi's obedience and humility in front of Shams forced his followers to also be humble and submissive. Rumi was no longer the Sheikh and the leader since Shams of Tabriz had taken over. Sometimes Shams even stood by the door and decided who would be permitted to see Rumi. Shams, who did not possess Rumi's eloquence, had become Rumi's tongue, and tolerating his harsh and offensive words became increasingly difficult for Rumi's disciples. Shams himself stated, "My words are similar to one from the grand skies and the people do not have the capacity for them." Still, Rumi's silence and acquiescence forced his followers to respect Shams as well. Some of Shams' stories and fables were later recited by Rumi as insightful poetry in the books of *Mathnavi* and some of Shams' thoughts were reflected in the book of *Divane Shams*.

Depending on the listener's view of Shams, his speeches either exasperated or stimulated them. Within these speeches,

Shams sometimes praised Rumi and sometimes praised himself, claiming that anyone who followed him would reach the level of perfection and he would "show God to them without any conjecture and speculation." This claim infuriated most of Rumi's students, since they considered Rumi's rank to be far above that of Shams. Despite his bitter and harsh words, Shams' lectures usually contained profound and interesting new revelations. One day, a scholar in front of Shams claimed that he could prove God's existence with definite reasoning and certainty. The following day, Shams sarcastically told him, "Last night I saw that the angels came to earth and were praising you because you have proven God's existence." Then he continued, "God is everlasting and is not in need of proof. The one whose existence should be proven is you." This type of bluntness and severity angered the majority of Rumi's supporters, but Rumi himself was fascinated and mesmerized by Shams. In front of Rumi, his followers treated Shams with kindness, but this courtesy was a mask that concealed their intense hatred. They were enraged and distraught that a strange vagabond had created a distance between them and their adored teacher and spiritual guide. Their animosity reached a point that some of the disciples cursed at Shams and threatened him with their swords. In secret, some students even intended to assassinate Shams.

Rumi was afraid of the possible consequences of his followers' animosity toward Shams and pleaded with Shams to ignore their objections and discourtesy. He would cry out, "You are the light of my house. Do not abandon me and leave me alone." The childish innocence apparent in the beautiful, magical sounds and words that he composed for Shams during that time is portrayed in some of the following verses:

(Divane Shams, 2054)

بشنیده ام که عزم سفر می کنی مکن
مهر حریف و یار دگر می کنی مکن

تو در جهان غریبی غربت چه می کنی
قصد کدام خسته جگر می کنی مکن

از ما مدزد خویش به بیگانگان مرو
دزدیده سوی غیر نظر می کنی مکن

ای مه که چرخ زیر و زبر از بر ای توست
ما را خراب وزیر و زبر می کنی مکن

...

I have heard that you are deciding to travel,
please don't.
You are desiring another friend and companion,
please don't.
You are a stranger in this world,
why are you acting strange?
Toward which tired soul are you aiming?
please don't.
Do not deprive us of yourself,
and do not go to strangers.
You are glancing toward others,
please don't.
Oh beautiful one,
the upper and lower part of the universe are for you.
You are destroying and turning us upside down,
please don't...

Shams' First Disappearance

Suddenly, without informing Rumi, Shams disappeared from Konya (1245; 643 HG). The news spread like wildfire from mouth to mouth among Rumi's followers. They felt that after fourteen months of suffering, they had been relieved from a catastrophe and had awakened from a terrible delirium. They believed that their long separation from their loving teacher and mentor was finally over. During that period, the theologians of the city and even the Sufis of the region had called Rumi misguided and lost. They had quoted their Sheikhs who had called Rumi an insane infidel and looked down on Samaa as a disgraceful new phenomenon. Now that Shams had left town, Rumi's disciples were hopeful that they would return to his sessions of preaching, teaching, and Koranic analysis. This wishful thinking caused flowers of hope to bloom in their hearts and minds. For Rumi, contrary to their thinking, Shams' departure was an overwhelming, unexpected disaster that shook him like thunder from the sky. Rumi felt that suddenly he had lost the sun in the daylight. In one fleeting moment, the light of his eyes, his hope for life, and the serenity of his heart had disappeared. Separation from Shams seemed unbearable to Rumi. He could not even imagine life without his spiritual guide, since Shams was everything to him. For Rumi, Shams epitomized love, hope, and life itself. Without Shams, he was completely alone and could not be content nor peaceful. When Rumi reflected on Shams, he envisioned a spiritual physician who had come from the unseen world through a long journey to relieve Rumi's soul from its dependency upon and affection for superficial knowledge and status. Now this holy healer had abandoned him, despite Rumi's need of his magical cure.

Not only did Rumi feel brokenhearted, but he also felt betrayed, since he was aware that his followers' dissatisfaction and anger toward Shams had forced him to leave Konya. From the day that Shams disappeared, Rumi remained in his house, alienating himself from the outside world and terminating all associations with his students and disciples. In his house, his wife and younger son were pleased. Only his older son was distressed and sorrowful due to Shams' disappearance and was sympathetic toward his father. Like Rumi, the twenty-one-year-old Sultan-Valad was fond of Shams and considered him his mentor. Rumi expressed his anguish only to Sultan-Valad and two of his close *Moreed* (disciples), Salah-uddin and Hosam-uddin, who were also suffering from Shams' departure. During those days of loneliness, Rumi did not see any one except his household and those faithful confidants.

Returning to speaking and lecturing seemed impossible to Rumi. During those days of silence and sadness, Rumi did not even recite or compose any poems since, without Shams, there was no pleasure in Samaa, music, or poetry. Witnessing Rumi's anguish, his followers became very remorseful regarding their treatment of Shams. They expressed their regrets through letters and messages, begged Rumi's forgiveness, and volunteered to search for Shams. Rumi accepted their apologies, but did not leave his seclusion. He was not ready to accept Shams' enemies as his companions, so he did not open his door, instead remaining hopeless and impatient in his isolation. Since he had lost Shams, peace and tranquility had left his heart and mind. Days and weeks passed. Silence and sorrow were Rumi's only true companions. This indicated to his supporters that to relieve Rumi and mend his broken heart, they must search for his beloved Shams without any further delay. However, Shams was like a bird. Throughout his life he had escaped from every dependency and temptation. Whenever he was threatened or bothered, he had flown to another strange place. This time he had flown away without leaving any address or trace. There was no clue to his whereabouts.

The Arrival of Shams' Letter

Finally, a traveler from Damascus brought a short letter from Shams that stated, "It should be known to Molana that this weak (man) is busy with good prayers for you and does not converse with any creature." Some researchers believe that around 120 days had passed from the day of Shams' sudden departure until the receipt of this letter. In his brief message, Shams prohibited Rumi from conversation with his followers. Although this was not clearly indicated, Rumi could discern that meaning from the letter. Even before receiving the letter, Rumi had separated himself from his students and supporters. Rumi was very eager to go to Damascus to see Shams, but his worries and grief had exhausted him to such an extent that he was not physically able to make the journey. After receiving the letter, Rumi composed the following Ghazal (verses in a special style of poetry) expressing his love and desire for Damascus:

(Divane Shams, 1493)

ما عاشق و سرگشته و شیدای دمشقیم
جان داده و دل بسته سودای دمشقیم

ز آن صبح سعادت که بتابید از آن سو
هر شام و سحر مست سحرهای دمشقیم

...

We love, desire, and long for Damascus,
We have given our soul and set our heart in desire of Damascus.
From that morning of fortune which shined from that direction,
Every evening and dawn we are intoxicated with Damascus' dawn...

Rumi wrote five or six letters in verse in which he expressed his desire in a respectful tone, attempting to reveal his

34

broken heart without causing Shams to become troubled. The subsequent is the most famous letter that Rumi sent to Shams:

(Divane Shams, 1760)

به خدایی که در ازل بودست   حی و دانا و قادر و قیوم

نور او شمعهای عشق فروخت   تا بشد صد هزار سر معلوم

از یکی حکم او جهان پر شد   عاشق وعشق و حاکم و محکوم

در طلسمات شمس تبریزی   گشت گنج عجایبش مکتوم

که از آن دَم که تو سفر کردی   از حلاوت جدا شدیم چو موم

همه شب همچو شمع میسوزیم   ز آتشش جفت وز انگبین محروم

در فراق جمال او ما را   جسم ویران و جان در و چون بوم

بی حضورت سماع نیست حلال   همچو شیطان طرب شده مرجوم

یک غزل بی تو هیچ گفته نشد   تا رسید آن مشرفهٔ مفهوم

پس بذوق سماع نامهٔ تو   غزلی پنج شش بشد منظوم

شام ما از تو صبح روشن باد   ای بتو فخر شام و اَرمَن و روم

(I swear) to God who has been from eternity,
Alive, knowledgeable, able, and most upstanding:
God's light lit the candles of love,
Then a hundred thousand mysteries were revealed.
From one of God's decrees, the world was filled,
With lovers and love, rulers and ruled.
From Shamse Tabriz' talismans,
The (God's) mysterious treasures became hidden.
From the moment that you departed,
We became separated from the honey like wax (honeycomb).
Every night we burn like a candle,
Fire is our companion, and deprived of (his) honey.
From separation of his beauty,
In the ruins of our body, our soul is like an owl.
Without your presence, Samaa is not Hallal (permissible),
Like Satan, joy has become expelled.
Without you even one Ghazal (poem) was not composed,
Till that letter was received.
In the enthusiasm of Samaa over your letter,
Five, six Ghazals were composed.

From you, our night became daybreak,
You are the pride of Shaam (Syria), Armenia, and Rome.

In another letter in the form of a beautiful Ghazal, Rumi expresses his longing and desire for Shams' return, as follows:

(Divane Shams, 2572)

جانا به غریبستان چندین به چه می مانی
بازآ تو از این غربت تا چند پریشانی

صد نامه فرستادم صد راه نشان دادم
یا راه نمی دانی یا نامه نمی خوانی

گر نامه نمی خوانی خود نامه تو را خواند
ور راه نمی دانی در پنجهٔ ره دانی

بازآ که در آن مَحبَس قدر تو نداند کَس
با سنگ دلان مَنشین چون گوهر این کانی

ای از دل و جان رَسته دست از دل و جان شُسته
از دام جهان جَسته بازآ که ز بازانی

هم آبی و هم جویی هم آب همی جویی
هم شیر و هم آهویی هم بهتر ازیشانی

چندست ز تو تا جان تو طرفه تری یا جان
آمیخته‌ای با جان یا پرتو جانانی

نور قمری در شب قند و شکری در لب
یا ربّ چه کسی یا ربّ اعجوبهٔ دورانی

هر دم ز تو زیب و فرّ از ما دل و جان و سر
بازار چنین خوشتر خوش بدهی و بستانی

36

از عشق تو جان بردن و ز ما چو شکر مردن
زهر از کف تو خوردن   سر چشمهٔ حیوانی

Oh my soul,
why are you staying so long in a strange place?
Please return from this strange place,
until when are you disheartened.
I sent a hundred letters,
I suggested a hundred ways;
You do not know the way,
or you do not read the letters.
If you are not reading the letter,
the letter is calling you,
And if you do not know the way,
knowing the way is in your palm.
Come back since, in that prison,
no one appreciates you,
Do not associate with stone hearts,
since you are the jewel of this treasure.
You are freed from heart and soul,
you have washed your hand from heart and soul;
You have escaped from the trap of the world,
come back since you are from the eagles.
You are the water and the stream,
you are also searching for water;
You are a lion and deer,
you are better than them.
You are the moonlight at night,
you are sweet and sugary to the lips,
Oh my creator, who is he (Shams)?
Oh my creator, you (Shams) are divine wonder.
Every moment from you, beauty and splendor,
from us, our heart, soul, and head;
Is there any bazaar better than this,
with such wonderful give and take?

In another Ghazal, Rumi explains his impatience and longing for
Shams' return:

به جان پاک تو ای معدن سخا و وفا
که صبر نیست مرا بی تو ای عزیز بیا

چه جای صبر که گر کوه قاف بود این صبر
ز آفتاب جدایی چو برف گشت فنا

...

I swear to your pure soul,
oh treasure of generosity and loyalty,
That I have no patience without you,
oh my dear, please come.
What a place for patience;
if this patience was Mount Ghaf,
From the sun of separation,
it would be annihilated like snow.

In another Ghazal during that period, Rumi again extols his love for Shams:

(Divane Shams, 2524)

اگر آب و گل ما را چو جان و دل پری بودی
به تبریز آمدی این دم بیابان را بپیمودی

بپر ای دل که پر داری برو انجا که بیماری
نماندی هیچ بیماری گر او رخسار بنمودی

If our water and soil had wings
like our soul and heart,
They would come to Tabriz
this moment and cross the desert.
Oh, my heart,
fly since you have wings,
Go there, since no illness would remain in an ill one,
if he (Shams) shows his face.

Sending for Shams

Finally, without waiting for a response to his letters, Rumi asked Sultan-Valad, his older son, to go to Damascus and, with humility and insistence, invite Shams to return to Konya. Rumi gave Sultan-Valad some cash and a short letter in the form of a poem. Although the letter was full of heartfelt affection and longing for Shams' return, its official and respectful tone was reminiscent of a student writing to his teacher with the acknowledgement of the teacher's high standing in the student's eyes. Rumi's words were written in a poetic form to indicate his love and yearning for Shams' companionship, which he had enjoyed during their Samaa and poetry sessions in their time of seclusion. Rumi also indicated in the letter that since Shams' departure he had not composed any poetry, hoping that this would demonstrate the sorrow and grief that resulted from his separation from Shams. The following poem in *Divane Shams* illustrates Rumi's instructions to his son and followers to bring Shams back to Konya. According to Dr. Foroozanfar, Rumi composed this Ghazal at the time of their departure and recited it for them in a loud voice.

(Divane Shams, 163)

بروید ای حریفان بکشید یار ما را
به من آورید آخر صنم گریز پا را

به ترانهای شیرین به بهانهای زرین
بکشید سوی خانه مه خوب خوش لقا را

اگر او به وعده گوید که دم دگر بیایم
همه وعده مکر باشد بفریبد او شما را

دم سخت گرم دارد که به جادویی و افسون
بزند گره بر آب او و ببندد او هوا را

39

بمبارکی و شادی چو نگار من در آید
بنشین نظاره می کن تو عجایب خدا را

چو جمال او بتابد چه بود جمال خوبان
که رُخ چو آفتابش بکشد چراغها را

برو ای دل سبک رو بیمن بدلبر من
برسان سلام و خدمت تو عقیق بی بها را

Oh friends,
go and bring our beloved,
Return to me at last the fleeing icon.
With sweet songs and golden excuses,
Pull toward the house the bright moon, the beautiful face.
If he promises that he will come in another moment,
All the promises are deceptions;
he will deceive you.
He has very warm breath that with magic and enchantment,
He could tie a knot on the water and catch the air.
When my beloved comes with jubilation and fortune,
Sit and observe God's wonders.
When his beauty shines,
what would be the beauty of the beautiful ones,
Since his face like the sun would diminish all the lamps?
Oh my heart,
go gently to my beloved in Yemen (famous for finest agates),
Give greetings and regards from this worthless agate.

In another Ghazal, Rumi proclaimed the following:

(Divane Shams, 900)

بگیر دامن لطفش که ناگهان بگریزد
ولی مکش تو چو تیرش که از کمان بگریزد

چه نقشها که ببازد چه حیلها که بسازد
بنقش حاضر باشد   ز راه جان بگریزد

بر آسمانش بجویی چو مه ز آب بتابد
در آب چونکه درآیی بر آسمان بگریزد

ز لامکانش بخوانی نشان دهد بمکانت
چو در مکانش بجویی به لامکان بگریزد
...

Grab onto his garb of mercy,
since he suddenly will flee;
Do not pull the arrow,
so he will flee from the bow.
What roles he will play,
what trickery he will make;
He'll be present in the body,
but will flee with the soul.
If you seek him in the sky,
he will shine in the water like the moonlight;
When you go to the water,
he will flee to the sky.
If you seek him beyond any place,
he will show you a place;
When you seek him in a place,
he will flee beyond any place...

The Return of Shams

After enduring a lengthy and strenuous journey, Sultan-Valad and approximately twenty of Rumi's followers arrived in Damascus. Sultan-Valad quickly found Shams after asking around and searching, since he knew the city from his years of studying there. He explained to Shams what had happened, expressed his father's torment and longing, and submitted the letter to him. He pleaded with humility to Shams to return to Konya and gave him the cash that Rumi had sent. The message brought a smile to Shams' lips, which was a mixture of satisfaction and shame. Shams protested with a combination of gratitude and disapproval, "Did Molana want to buy me with this gold?" Immediately, he added that Rumi's hinting would have been sufficient and there was no need for other things. Shams accepted Sultan-Valad's invitation on behalf of Rumi and his disciples, and decided to return with them. However, when they reached Halab on their way to Konya, Shams became hesitant. At that point, he might have thought that his return would not be beneficial. Sultan-Valad reiterated their needs and depicted the overwhelming love, desire, and restlessness of Rumi and the others. He insisted that they should continue traveling toward Konya. During the whole journey, while Shams was riding, Sultan-Valad was walking beside him as a sign of modesty and respect. This was also an expression of extreme appreciation in order to remove any traces of hurt or disappointment that might have remained in Shams' memory and mind. He hoped that this homage would please Shams and encourage him to continue the trip. During their month-long journey, Rumi was impatiently burning with the fire of longing and desire. This intense yearning had actually lasted three months, from the time Sultan-Valad left until he returned to Konya with Shams.

The reception for Shams was extraordinary. Sultan-Valad had sent a messenger to inform Rumi about their arrival and, besides Rumi's supporters, Sufi and Akhiyan groups had also come outside of Konya's gate to greet and welcome Shams. Rumi's excitement and exultation were so intense that he spontaneously composed some beautiful, stirring love poems signifying his great exhilaration and joy. The following is an example of Rumi's expression of happiness:

(Divane Shams, 58)

رسید آن شه رسید آن شه بیارایید ایوان را
فرو برید ساعدها برای خوب کنعان را

چو آمد جان جان جان   نشاید برد نام جان
به پیشش جان چه کار آید مگر از بهر قربان را

بدم بی عشق گمراهی درآمد عشق ناگاهی
بدم کوهی شدم کاهی برای اسب سلطان را

هلا یاران که بخت آمد گه ایثار رخت آمد
سلیمانی بتخت آمد برای عزل شیطان را

...

The king arrived,
the king arrived,
beautify the terrace,
Bend your hands for the noble of Canaan (Joseph).
Since the dearest of the dears of soul came,
It is not proper to mention even life.
What use will life be before him,
Except to sacrifice it for him?
I was lost without love,
suddenly love came;
I was a mountain,
I became a straw for the horse of the king.
Hail, oh friend,
that good luck came,
it's the time to sacrifice your worldly belongings,
Since Solomon came to the throne for toppling Satan.

After greeting everyone, Shams and Sultan-Valad went to Rumi's house. When Rumi saw Shams, he embraced him and felt as if no separation existed between their souls. Rumi became delighted, ecstatic, and inspired again and returned to his followers. Friends and supporters rejoiced on the occasion of Shams' return. They celebrated and held Samaa sessions and no one thought of eating or sleeping. Rumi was so exhilarated that he enthusiastically and spontaneously recited and composed verses. During this time, Sultan-Valad, like Rumi, was demonstrating his love and spiritual affection for Shams. Shams, in his conversations with Rumi, talked about the memories of the journey from Damascus to Konya and praised Sultan-Valad with kind words. This increased Rumi's love for his son even more. His younger son, Ala-uddin, did not participate in those celebrations and Shams' praise of his older brother added to his hostility toward Shams.

In the meantime, Shams had become fond of Keymia Khatoon, Rumi's stepdaughter. When Shams proposed marriage to Keymia, it was immediately accepted, since this guaranteed that Shams would remain for a longer period of time in Konya. Even though he was over sixty years old, the thought of marriage had never crossed Shams' mind, since he had always detached himself from all dependencies. Now, however, he was experiencing a new form of love, a love between a man and a woman. Whatever those long journeys throughout the world and conversations with Sheikhs and scholars had not taught him, this new love was teaching him. From this love, he learned new and different things. Keymia brought him down to earth and offered him a distinct kind of tranquility and peace. This relationship also made him more sociable and connected to the physical world.

Shams' Second Disappearance With No Return

Three days after a mysterious illness, Keymia suddenly passed from this world and started her new life and journey in a higher world (1248; 645 HG). Shams' marriage had lasted only six months, and, after her passing, he became very disheartened and mournful. He lost his peace and tranquility. Staying in Rumi's house, which had become their residence after their marriage, became very painful. After so many years of wandering and drifting, for a few months he had tried to establish some roots under the light of Keymia's love. Shams also believed that Rumi had no need for him anymore. He had climbed up the ladder of enlightenment and freed himself from the glory and grandeur of his previous position and status. Rumi was on his way to soar to the peak of his potential. Essentially, Shams' task had been successfully accomplished. Except for the dependency of loving Shams, nothing else could prevent Rumi from his wonderful high-flying journey. For Shams himself, leaving Konya meant leaving painful memories and the loss of Keymia. Furthermore, he did not want to become another obstacle in Rumi's path by creating a new dependency for him. For about a week, he was very pensive, thinking about himself, Rumi, and the unbelievable experiences that he had faced in the past few months, particularly his marriage to Keymia. To free himself from this last desire and the pain of Keymia's memory, he had to leave everything behind one more time in order to once again find himself and become free of any dependency.

Suddenly, Shams disappeared again without a trace. Some researchers believe that Shams was killed by some of Rumi's supporters who again conspired against him. It seemed that after Shams' return to Konya, the same resentment and jealousy as before resurfaced again among Rumi's followers. Soon they forgot their expressions of regret and repentance to Rumi in regards to Shams after his first departure. Aflaaki stated that one day someone called Shams. When he went outside the house, he faced seven people. One of them hit him with a dagger. Jaami confirmed this story and added that after being injured by the dagger, Shams recited a prayer and all his assailants fell unconscious. After they returned to consciousness, Shams had vanished and only a few drops of blood remained. It has been stated that Shams' disappearance took place in 1248 (645 HG). Some also stated that Rumi's son, Ala-uddin, was an accomplice in the killing of Shams and that he was buried in an unknown well. Despite this theory, there is not much historical certainty about Shams' assassination or Ala-uddin's participation. It is known that when Ala-uddin died after a severe illness (1260; 658 HG) Rumi did not attend his funeral, choosing instead to go to the gardens outside of Konya due to his anger and dissatisfaction with Ala-uddin. According to Dr. Schimmel, it is likely that after Shams was stabbed and thrown in a well, Sultan-Valad was informed about the crime and subsequently took the body out of the well and quickly buried it nearby, covering the tomb with plaster and earth. Dr. Schimmel has stated that recent excavations by Mehmet Önder, the former director of the Mevlâna Müzesi in Konya, have proven the existence of a large tomb from the Seljuk period covered with plaster on the site of Shams' *Magham* (memorial). Still, the only definite historical fact regarding this mysterious episode is that Shams vanished and never returned again.

The rumor of Shams' death spread throughout the city. When Rumi heard the rumor, he went to the roof of his house. As he was sadly and sorrowfully pacing, he recited the following poem:

(Divane Shams, Rubaiyat 806)

کی گفت که آن زنده جاوید بمرد
کی گفت که آفتاب امید بمرد

آن دشمن خورشید در آمد بر بام
دو دیده ببست وگفت خورشید بمرد

Who said that everlasting living died?
Who said that the sun of hope died?

The enemy of the sun came to the roof,
Closed his two eyes, and said the sun died.

Shams had ignited a fire inside most of Rumi's supporters, and until that fire was extinguished, no one felt safe and peaceful. Some researchers believe that Shams' real motive for his final desertion was to flee from his tender memories of Keymia. This was Shams' last temptation, which had trapped him and caused him to lose his freedom. By leaving, he would regain his freedom and no longer be dependent on anything, so he would be free at last.

48

CHAPTER 3

THE MYSTERY OF SHAMS,

THE

ETERNAL BIRD

Shams' appearances and disappearances in Konya occurred over a two-year period, but the memory of Shams remained in Rumi's mind and writings forever. From Shams' own statements and other researchers' stories, it is evident that Shams left his father's house at an early age. His father, Ali Ebne Malekdad Tabrizi, was apparently a righteous man. After leaving home, Shams traveled in the tradition of Sufis. In Tabriz, he became a disciple of Sheikh Abubakr Salehbaaf, but left him after awhile. It has been stated that Shams had taught, "The Sheikh has drunkenness from God, but does not have the awareness which comes after." In his search during the long years of his extensive journeys, which took him from Khorasan to Iraq and Syria, he had met other Sheikhs, possibly Rokn-uddin Sajaasi and Baba Kamal Jondi, but as their conversations did not result in any spiritual progress for him, he left them, too. He had also met Sheikh Ohadd-uddin Kermani and Mohiy-uddin Ebne Arabi, but did not feel any attraction toward them. Later in Konya, he stated that his meeting with Ebne Arabi was not as beneficial to him as his encounter and discussions with Rumi. Shams had not become a disciple of any of those Sheikhs and had not requested to receive a *Khergheh* (the dervish frock or robe) from them. He had claimed that he had received his Khergheh from the Prophet Mohammad, peace and blessing be upon him, in his dreams.

Shams was opposed to pretending to be virtuous, or to relating himself to any Sufi dynasty and Khergheh. Despite the fact that he was considered a Sufi and a theologian, throughout his traveling he did not stay in the Khaneghahs or religious schools. Instead, as he stated himself, he stayed in the caravanserai (caravan houses) frequented by strangers. In the small rooms of the caravanserai, he slept on a rush-mat, ate very little, and concealed his poverty. Whenever anyone discovered the truth about his status, he disappeared from that city and traveled elsewhere. Sometimes he worked as a simple laborer to earn his daily bread, occasionally disappearing after the job was finished but before receiving his wages. Evidently, he would not accept wages from just anyone. Occasionally he wove cummerbunds in the caravanserai to earn his livelihood, and in some provinces, like Arzanalrum, he taught children. Shams always tried to conceal his state of affairs. His demeanor was apparently very similar to that of the *Malamatiyyan*, a group of mystics who purposefully denigrated and demeaned themselves in others' eyes. The Malamatiyyan had recognized that Sufis could sacrifice everything except their good name. For this reason, they intentionally tried to defame themselves and did not seek recognition and respect. They believed that, by tarnishing their reputation, they could release themselves from the imprisonment of fame and self-promotion, the major obstacle to spiritual evolvement and progress. They wanted to free themselves from this last chain and shackle. Hafez, another famous Persian poet and mystic, specifically referred to the Malamatiyyan belief in his superb poetry.

Shams did not associate with ordinary Sufis and openly stated, "In this world, I have no business with the ordinary; I have not come for them. Those who are the leaders in this world, I put my finger over their veins." Thus, it is evident from his statements that Shams had come to Konya to search for Rumi. He must have heard about Rumi's circumstances and situation and recognized him as one of those scholarly guides. Shams had appeared to put his hand over Rumi's vein and cure his illness of arrogance and ambition. He had acknowledged many times that he did not have one hundredth of Rumi's knowledge. In response to Rumi's praise of him, he stated, "A hundred thousand like Shams are not even a particle from Rumi's grandeur."

Through his years of experience and searching, Shams had concluded that Samaa was the way to unveil the cover between man and God and lead to reunion with God. He also believed that abandoning falsehoods opened up the opportunity for one to reunite with God. His method was basically summarized in these two teachings. In his opinion, discarding falsehoods would prevent a human being who was seeking God from becoming involved in philosophical arguments or yielding to the Sufis' traditional ideas or to those who falsely claim divine leadership.

The spiritual connection and attraction between a drifter from Tabriz and a theologian, scholar, and preacher who was Konya's religious authority epitomized what the Sufis call the *old relation* among spirits. During their encounters and conversations, Rumi had gradually become one with Shams. This was a divine reunification. Rumi learned through this spiritual reunion that the highest human perfection does not lie in trying to save oneself. He discovered that those who are righteous and devout and the Sufis who seek that perfection through self-purification and disconnection of desires only save themselves from waves of disasters, but do not find a way toward perfection. Human perfection is not even found in the efforts of the scholars, preachers, and learned ones who try to save other drowning individuals and guide the lost ones. Instead, perfection lies in setting foot outside of self, beyond the limited world of people, and in connecting and reuniting with the whole universe.

Rumi's Unsuccessful Search for Shams

As Sultan-Valad later stated, "Shams' disappearance and departure carried Rumi to the border of insanity." The intensity of Rumi's immersion in poetry and Samaa after Shams' departure epitomized his spiritual upheaval. In contrast to Rumi's behavior after Shams' first disappearance, this time he did not remain in seclusion or choose silence. He saw Shams in the poetry and Samaa, but grew impatient at his physical absence. Konya lost its peace and calm in Rumi's fervor, Samaa, and restlessness. The verses that Rumi composed during that time, which continuously repeat Shams' name, indicate his pain at the separation and longing for reunion. For weeks and then months, he eagerly awaited Shams' return. Rumi asked any traveler who entered the city about Shams and continuously searched for any trace of him. He was happy to see and reward anyone who would give him any news, true or false. One day a man told him that he had seen Shams in Damascus. Rumi did not have any cash with him, so he gave his clothes and shoes as a reward to the man. After the informant departed, another person told Rumi that this was false news and that the man had not even traveled to Damascus. Rumi replied, "For his false news I gave him my clothes; if his news was true, I would have given him my life instead." Nevertheless, at that time Rumi was drowned in the fervor of Samaa and was not yet ready to travel to find Shams. From Rumi's continuous dance, Samaa, and passion, his companions were exhausted. He had composed numerous Ghazals, pouring all of his ardor and love into those verses until they filled several notebooks. Still, there was no trace of Shams and Rumi gradually lost hope that Shams was hiding in Konya, as he originally had suspected. Some people told him that Shams might be in Syria. Subsequently, Rumi decided to go to Syria in search of Shams.

(Divane Shams, 2186)

خداوندا چو تو صاحب قرآن کو
برابر با مکان تو مکان کو

53

کسی که او گفت دیدم شمس دین را
سؤالش کن که راه آسمان کو

زبان و جان من با وصل او رفت
بشرح خاک تبریزم زبان کو

...

*Ask from the one who said I saw Shams-uddin (Sun of
Religion)*
Where is the way to the heaven?
My tongue and soul left with his union,
Where is a tongue to describe my soil of Tabriz? ...

Since he was doubtful that this time his son and supporters
would be able to bring Shams back to Konya, Rumi decided to
make the journey personally and began preparing to travel to
Damascus. Sultan-Valad and all of his close disciples
accompanied him. This was a strenuous trip, since internal
conflicts in Syria made traveling dangerous. In Damascus, Rumi
started Samaa sessions, in the hope of attracting Shams or people
who might have associated with him. These gatherings attracted
many Farsi-speaking people and other Sufis. Some of Rumi's
verses in Arabic are reminiscent of that time in Damascus.
Shams was not found in the city, but the city found a wonderful
fervor and joyfulness due to Rumi's presence and his Samaa
sessions. Also, the story of the search for the spiritually loved
Sun of Tabriz was whispered from mouth to mouth throughout
the town. The account of this fervent love, which had forced a
learned scholar and theologian like Rumi to search for a
nameless vagabond dervish, must have seemed extraordinary to
the residents of Damascus. They must have been inspired by
Rumi's intense passion and desire for his mystical companion.
Nonetheless, because of the unstable and difficult situation in
Damascus and the fruitlessness of their search, Rumi and his
entourage were eventually forced to return to Konya, even more
exhausted and fatigued than before. The next verses are about
that time:

(Divane Shams, 1568)

ای جان لطیف و ای جهانم
از خواب گرانت بر جهانم

بی شرم و حیا کنم تقاضا
دانی که غریبم بی امانم

بسیار شبست کاندرین دشت
من از پی باج راهبانم

همخانه گریخت از نفیرم
همسایه گریخت از فغانم

...

Oh, my elegant soul and oh my world,
From your deep sleep I am in this world.
With no shame and shyness, I seek,
You know that I am a stranger and restless...
It has been many nights in this field,
I was guarding the road in search of tribute.
The housemate fled from my cries,
The neighbor ran away from my lament.

Still, the hope of finding Shams in Konya or at least receiving some message or letter as before was alive in Rumi's heart. After his return to Konya, Rumi once again drowned himself in music, poetry, and Samaa. Burning in the fire of Shams' love, and in remembrance of Shams, Rumi composed some of his most exciting verses with the most loving and passionate tone. He sang some of these exquisite love poems as he turned with the beautiful Samaa music. After a while, Rumi started thinking of taking a second trip to Syria. The thought of traveling to Tabriz also passed through his mind, but there is no historical certainty that he went there. However, it is evident that he did travel to Syria one more time. This time he also found Damascus void of Shams and, after staying there for a while with no result, he returned to Konya. When his hope of finding Shams dwindled, he loudly recited the following Ghazal:

(From Divane Shams, according to Afzal Iqbal)

چند کنم ترا طلب خانه به خانه در به در
چند گریزی از برم گوشه به گوشه کو به کو

How long should I seek you
house to house,
door to door?
How long are you escaping from me
from corner to corner,
from street to street? ...

If Rumi heard rumors that a corpse was discovered that could be Shams, he would reject that news. This is apparent from one of the Ghazals:

(Divane Shams, 1994)

بشنو از بوالهوسان قصهَ میرعسان
رندی از حلقه ما گشت در این کوی نهان

مدتی هست که ما در طلبش سوخته ایم
شب و روز از طلبش هر طرفی‌جامه در ان

...

گر چنان کشته شوی زندهٔ جاوید شوی
خدمت از جان چنین کشته بتبریز رسان

Listen to the fickle people,
about the story of the sentry leader,
A lover from our circle
has disappeared in this alley.
It is a while,
that we have been burned in his desire,
Day and night searching everywhere,

tearing our clothes...
If you get killed this way,
you become alive forever,
Deliver greetings to Tabriz from such a slayed soul.

Finally after endless searches, Rumi did not see Shams' face anywhere and realized that what he was searching for was actually living inside himself. Rumi understood that he was asking for signs and traces of Shams from others needlessly, because Shams was incredibly alive within him. Shams' departure with no return was a necessary cure for Rumi, since Rumi would have been caught in another trap if their companionship had continued. The dependency that he felt for Shams would have been a great obstacle on his journey of discovery on the majestic path of love, a journey that involved abandoning all material dependencies to reach a step-by-step dissolution of self into the Divine Creator. Rumi had come a long way from his childhood in Balkh all the way to Konya and the meeting with Shams and the consequences of his companionship and departure. During that period, Rumi had learned the essence of Shams' teaching, which consisted of two steps:

1. *Tabattol* - to step outside of your worldly dependencies and desires.

2. *Fanaa* - to step outside of yourself totally.

(Mathnavi Book 3, Verse 4235)

پایه پایه تا ملاقات خدا   از مقامات تَبَتُّل تا فَنا

From the state of Tabattol to Fanaa,
Step by step to meet God.

After Rumi's last return to Konya, his only desire was to immerse himself totally in Samaa, music, and poetry. Returning to preaching and teaching was impossible for him. He did not have any desire to issue religious decrees (Fatwas) for which he was occasionally asked. The fervor and passion of Samaa had completely captured his existence. In his seclusion, he played the rebeck (a pear shaped stringed musical instrument). His love was also transferred into the making of the rebeck, which he infused with his own ingenuity and design.

CHAPTER 4

RUMI'S FIRST KHALIFEH

SALAH-UDDIN ZARKOOB

One day, Rumi and his followers were passing through the goldsmith bazaar. The sound of hammers striking anvils resonated throughout the marketplace. Suddenly, an incredible passion and exultation came over Rumi and he started to turn fervently. Some of his companions also joined him. This spontaneous Samaa occurred in front of Salah-uddin's shop, who was working with his laborers inside. When Salah-uddin saw Rumi's jubilation, he instructed the workers to continue striking the anvils. People in the bazaar were astonished to see Rumi's passion and dance. Salah-uddin's employees became tired and sweat poured from their bodies, but Salah-uddin directed them to continue nonstop. Then he came out from the store and joined Rumi in Samaa. He instructed the workers, "As long as Molana is turning and or doing Samaa, do not cease striking the anvils, and if the gold is wasted there is no problem."

The elderly Salah-uddin joined Rumi and turned enthusiastically and blissfully, step by step with him. Rumi and Salah-uddin were communicating love and spirituality through the language of Samaa. Rumi had been turning and dancing from noon until the next prayer time (the prayer before sunset). By this time, the gold from Salah-uddin's shop had been smashed into pieces, spreading all over the shop and outside. Finally Salah-uddin, who had lost all of his energy and did not have enough endurance to keep up with Rumi, left the circle with humility and apologies. Rumi stopped after a few moments as a sign of respect for Salah-uddin. Salah-uddin, in a drunken revelry caused by his fervor and excitation, gave away all the gold, cash, and equipment in his shop to his laborers and bystanders who had gathered around Rumi and watched their Samaa. This generous sacrifice, which was a sign of "freedom from self," taught Rumi's entourage a great lesson of generosity and freedom. Salah-uddin had lost his self in this spiritual experience and successfully shed all material dependencies as if he were merely removing a robe. Rumi composed the following famous Ghazal, which refers to this experience in the goldsmith shop:

(Divane Shams, 2515)

یکی گنجی پدید آمد در آن دکان زر کوبی
زهی صورت زهی معنی زهی خوبی زهی خوبی

...

A treasure was discovered in that goldsmith shop,
What a fine face,
what a fine meaning,
what a fine goodness,
what a fine goodness. ...

For many years, Salah-uddin had been a disciple, admirer, and close confidant of Rumi who had frequently participated in his Samaa sessions with love and enthusiasm. With this new experience, Rumi found in Salah-uddin a new reflection of Shams that Rumi thought he had lost. This time, Rumi's love for Shams, which was love toward Allah, humanity, and the whole universe, became manifested through Salah-uddin's existence. Despite the fact that Rumi, after years of searching for Shams, had discovered Shams inside himself, now the elderly Salah-uddin had become like a mirror reflecting Shams' image. From the time of his last return from Damascus, Rumi's followers had wanted him to guide them as their Sheikh. Rumi, due to his spiritual circumstances and upheaval, was not in the mood to be involved with his followers. Thus he chose Salah-uddin as his *Khalifeh* (successor) after the goldsmith bazaar event. Rumi even told his son, Sultan-Valad, to follow Salah-uddin as his Sheikh and leader. Due to his love for Salah-uddin, Rumi also married Salah-uddin's daughter Fatimeh to Sultan-Valad. In those days, Rumi was intoxicated with passion and fervor, doing Samaa for hours and days and outlasting most of his followers. Salah-uddin stated, "I do not have the endurance of his lordship Rumi." For this reason, during the lengthy Samaa sessions, Salah-uddin stayed in a corner and became drowned in Rumi's dance with passionate excitement and the revelry of jubilation and exultation. It was during this time that Rumi, in one of his intoxicated Ghazals, used Salah-uddin's name at the beginning of the verses, and not at the end as was customary. There are at least seventy-one Ghazals in which Rumi mentions Salah-uddin's name. The following is one:

(Divane Shams, 1805)

پوشیده چون جان می روی اندر میان جان من
سرو خرامان منی   ای رونق بستان من

چون می روی بی من مرو ای جان جان ای تن مرو
و از چشم من بیرون مشو ای مشعلهَ تابان من

هفت آسمان را بردرم و از هفت دریا بگذرم
چون دلبرانه بنگری در جان سرگردان من

تا آمدی اندر برم   شد کفر و ایمان چاکرم
ای دیدن تو دین من   وی روی تو ایمان من

بی پا و سر کردی مرا بی خواب و خور کردی مرا
در پیش یعقوب اندرآ   ای یوسف کنعان من

از لطف تو چون جان شدم وز خویشتن پنهان شدم
ای هست تو پنهان شده   در هستی پنهان من
...
ای شَه صلاح الدّین من   ره دان من   ره بین من
ای فارغ از تمکین من   ای برتر از امکان من

You are going hidden,
like the soul inside my life,
You are my dancing cypress,
You are the light of my garden.
Since you are going,
do not go without me,
Oh dear soul,
do not go without body,
Do not go out of my sight,
oh my shining torch,

62

I tear the seven skies,
and I pass from the seven seas,
When you look lovingly at my stray soul.
Since you embraced me,
blasphemy and faith became my servants,
Oh, seeing you my religion,
oh your image my faith.
You made me without feet and head,
you made me lose my sleep and appetite,
Come to Jacob,
oh my Joseph of Canaan.
From your love I became alive,
and became hidden from myself,
Your existence is hidden in my unseen existence.
Oh my king, Salah-uddin,
the knower of my path and the seer of my path,
Oh needless of my obedience,
oh beyond my limits.

Salah-uddin was born in a village near Konya called Kaameleh. Initially, he worked as a farmer and fisherman. Later, in his youth he came to Konya to work in a goldsmith shop. After many years of working in the bazaar as a goldsmith, he acquired a shop, some workers, and a garden outside of Konya, which was a resting and gathering place for his family and friends. As mentioned earlier, after giving away everything that he had in the store, Salah-uddin left his profession and business as a goldsmith. He also prepared provisions for Samaa gatherings. Gradually, Salah-uddin became poor to the point that, when his younger daughter, Hadiyeh, married, he needed Rumi's help to prepare her dowry. Salah-uddin had sacrificed his wealth to pursue Rumi and his path.

Accepting Salah-uddin as a Sheikh and Rumi's Khalifeh (successor) was very difficult for Rumi's disciples, especially since they had known Salah-uddin as a simple farmer and goldsmith and not a literate and learned scholar like Rumi. They considered him to be a simple good-natured commoner with whom they had conversed in the mosque and bazaar. According to them, he did not possess any special talent, knowledge, or scholarly ability. Rumi's love and respect for Salah-uddin made his followers jealous and unhappy. This dissatisfaction and jealousy increased to the point that a conspiracy arose against Salah-uddin, seemingly a repetition of Shams' earlier predicament.

The elderly Salah-uddin was not an orator by any means and his pronunciation of *Namaz* (the five required daily prayers) was not very exact. If the followers asked him a question about theology, sometimes he did not know the answer. He also spoke in the dialect of the bazaar people and at times mispronounced words in the manner of the common people. These issues were the cause of envy and anger among Rumi's disciples, particularly since Salah-uddin now had become an intermediary between them and Rumi. Rumi insisted that the essence of Namaz was not in pronunciation or the apparent basis, but instead lay in the passion and desire of the heart, which was the soul of the Namaz and above the obvious. In a verse later in *Mathnavi*, Rumi refers to the fact that in the path of love, the essential matters are not the classical and official knowledge with which most people are concerned:

(Mathnavi, Book 2, Verse 159)

دفتر صوفی سواد و حرف نیست
جز دل اسپید همچون برف نیست

The Sufis' book is not the knowledge and the words,
It is a heart, pure, and white like snow.

Salah-uddin's situation is also later reflected in *Mathnavi* in the story of holy Moses (peace and blessings be upon him) and the shepherd. In this story, Moses scolded the shepherd because he was praying and talking to God in a simple and crude manner that did not meet holy Moses' approval. Later in the story, a revelation comes from God to Moses that the shepherd's sincerity and earnestness were more important than the manner in which the prayer was offered.

64

When Rumi learned about the conspiracy against Salah-uddin, he became disappointed and saddened and for a while did not allow any of his supporters in his presence. Salah-uddin's calm and patience and Rumi's objections resulted in the repentance and apology of the disciples and acceptance of Salah-uddin as a Sheikh and Rumi's Khalifeh. Rumi also encouraged his son to respect Salah-uddin and be considerate of his wife, Salah-uddin's daughter. Rumi loved and cared for Salah-uddin so much that, after many years, he held a preaching session at Salah-uddin's request like the ones prior to meeting Shams.

During the ten years (1249-1259; 647-657 HG) that Salah-uddin was Rumi's Khalifeh, Sultan-Valad stated, "They were like one soul in two bodies." A relative calm appeared after the wearisome search for Shams had ended. Rumi had found in Salah-uddin the talent and ability of a Sheikh like Bayazid or Kharaghaani (two renowned Sufi masters). Toward the end of his life, Salah-uddin was ill and exhausted, mainly resting in bed. He suffered from old age, frailty and pain, especially pain in his fingernails due to inflammation. Rumi was very saddened and distressed due to his suffering and visited him daily, sitting by his bed and trying to comfort him. Finally, Salah-uddin passed away (January 1259; Moharram 657 HG). As he had requested, his funeral procession was mixed with the sounds of the tambourine and drum and Rumi turned and danced with his entourage while Salah-uddin was carried to the graveyard and buried next to Rumi's father. During those years, Rumi composed many poems for Salah-uddin. He composed verses for him while he was ill, at his funeral, and in painful reminiscence of him after his departure to the next world. Those beautiful verses are found in *Divane Shams*. In particular, in the next beautiful Ghazal he commemorates the loss of Salah-uddin:

(Divane Shams, 2364)

ای ز هجرانت زمین و آسمان بگریسته
دل میان خون نشسته عقل و جان بگریسته

65

چون به عالم نیست یک کس مر مکانت را عوض
در عزای تو مکان و لامکان بگریسته
...

From your separation,
The earth and the sky have wept,
The heart has sat in the midst of the blood;
the wisdom and soul have wept.
Since in the world,
there is no one to replace you,
In your mourning,
place and no-place have wept. ...

CHAPTER 5

RUMI'S TRUE SAMAA

Rumi's "true Samaa" was different from the Samaa of other ordinary Sufis which had become common in those days. To Rumi, Samaa was a spiritual passion and fervor. The essential condition for Rumi's Samaa was to have an empty stomach. In this kind of Samaa, under the influence of music, poetry, and dance, the participants became so excited and ecstatic that they tore their robes, made a drunken uproar, turned for hours in front of each other or with each other, and emptied themselves of their individual selves. They opened their hands and feet in their desire to soar beyond the earthly world. It seemed that they were defying gravity, whirling with amazing lightness and elegance. In their angelic spinning they removed all worldly bonds. In Rumi's Samaa sessions, the participants would continuously turn, reaching a blazing fire of euphoria from the passion and excitement. Rumi saw Samaa as a tool to achieve freedom. He believed that Samaa would help the soul free itself from whatever had trapped it in the world of material possessions and sensations and then aid it, step by step, to soar to the divine eternity.

In general, Samaa is heavy with symbolism. Dancers whirl with their right arms extended to the sky and their left arms to the ground. Grace is received from Allah and distributed to humanity and every living creature on the Earth. The dancers themselves represent the planets circling the sun, who is their spiritual leader, the Morad or Sheikh. Similarly, every electron and proton is spinning around their nucleus, as the heavenly bodies spin around the sun. Rumi refers to this spiritual dance in *Mathnavi* in the following manner:

(Mathnavi, Book 3, starting from Verse 95)

رقص آنجا کن که خود را بشکنی   پنبه را از ریش شهوت برکنی
رقص و جولان بر سر میدان کنند   رقص اندر خون خود مردان کنند
چون رهند ازدست خود دستی زنند   چون جهند ازنقص خود رقصی کنند
مطربانشان از درون دف می زنند   بحرها در شورشان کف می زنند
تو نبینی لیک بهر گوششان   برگ ها بر شاخ ها هم کف زنان
تو نبینی برگ ها را کف زدن   گوش دل باید نه این گوش بدن

Dance where you can break yourself,
And separate the cotton (purity) from the wound of lust.
They dance and turn in the battlefield;
(Righteous) Men dance in their own blood.
When they escape from themselves,
they clap their hands;
When they flee from their faults,
then they dance.
Inside them, the musicians play tambourine;
Oceans in their ecstasy break into foam.
You do not see, but for their ears,
The leaves on the branches are also clapping.
You do not see the leaves clapping,
This requires the spiritual ear, not the physical ear.

(Mathnavi, Book 4, starting from Verse 742)

كه در او باشد خيال اجتماع   پس غذای عاشقان آمد سماع

بلكه صورت گردد از بانگ و صفير   قوتی گيرد خيالات ضمير

آنچنان كه آتش آن جوز ريز   آتش عشق از نواها گشت تيز

Therefore, Samaa became the food for lovers,
Therein lies the dream of reunion.
The mental fantasies gather strength,
They become images from tune and sound.
The love fire became inflamed from the melodies...

The other theologians of Rumi's time had a low opinion of Samaa and compared it to hedonistic practices. Therefore, they were constantly scolding and blaming Rumi for doing Samaa, which they considered to be a new and false phenomenon that would cause corruption and spread falsehoods. They also instigated both ordinary and powerful people against Rumi and his entourage. Once Rumi sent them a message stating, "I left whatever was related to the glory, position, and grandeur of the scholars and theologians. Since the poor rebeck was not favored in our time, our hospitality caused us to be receptive of it. But if you think that the rebeck also would be beneficial for you the

69

learned ones, I would be happy to leave that also to you." This was a frank and straightforward response, which stunned the theologians, who did not dare to even respond. Rumi's opponents, with the pretense of caring about him, were saying, "What a pity that a dear learned man and a prince suddenly became insane and from the continuation of Samaa, hardship, and hunger lost his mind." Calling him a prince referred to his father's title of Sultan al Olamah (King of the Learned Ones).

In Rumi's world, Samaa was not useless jubilation and forgetfulness. It was spiritual meditation and self-discipline. His followers also viewed Samaa as similar to the prayer of pious people. In their belief, prayer was a connection between man and God, and the true Samaa was no different. In fact, during Samaa, the verses read were all related to a beautiful and humble communication with the Almighty which, combined with their loving passion and fervor, would help them shed the veils of desire and self. They were continuously chanting the names of Allah and the Prophet Mohammad and sending peace and blessings. Samaa was so holy for Rumi that he would delay it only for Namaz (the five required daily prayers). Even when Rumi was drowned in Samaa and exultation, if someone reminded him that it was the time for the daily prayer, he would stop Samaa and start the Namaz.

Samaa sessions were usually held in Rumi's school or his confidants' houses, and people who were unfamiliar with the traditions of the true Samaa were not permitted to enter. Once in a while, if a stranger happened to enter their sessions, they treated him with respect and tolerated him as much as possible, endeavoring to be sensitive to his feelings. Once, a man drunk with alcohol came to their Samaa session. During the dance, he became excited and, in drunken revelry, began hitting Rumi, who was in his spiritual trance state. Several times, Rumi's entourage tried to warn him and, when he started to shout loudly, they grabbed him. However, Rumi forbade them from disturbing the drunken man, stating, "He has drunk the wine and you are acting drunk."

CHAPTER 6

RUMI'S SECOND KHALIFEH

HOSAM-UDDIN

Five years after Salah-uddin's death, Rumi designated Hosam-uddin as his Khalifeh (successor) to succeed Salah-uddin (1264; 662 HG). Hosam-uddin was born in Konya (1225; 622 HG). As stated earlier, he had joined Rumi's entourage as a young man in the early years of Rumi's arrival in Konya. He was one of the few loyal confidants who had loved Shams from the beginning. Hosam-uddin's father was Akhi Turk Armavi, who was a leader of the Akhiyan group and had a considerable number of followers. After Hosam-uddin's father's death, his father's group looked to him as their leader. When Hosam-uddin became Rumi's disciple, his followers also became Rumi's supporters.

Unlike Salah-uddin, Hosam-uddin was literate and knowledgeable, in addition to being blessed with a pleasing voice. Since he was a powerful and capable person, Hosam-uddin was placed in charge of looking after the affairs of Rumi's followers. During these times, numerous people from all different classes of society - from rich to poor, prominent to needy - would come every day to see Rumi. Rumi dictated many letters to Hosam-uddin addressed to the important and powerful people in the region at the request of needy people who came to him and asked for help with their problems. At this point in his life, Rumi had reached a wonderful state of peace and serenity. When he was not in the presence of disciples and friends, his time was occupied with continual fasting, ablution, the true Samaa, and passionate, fervent Namaz. This resulted in countless spiritual discoveries and visions.

During his absence, Rumi's followers in their gatherings recited poetry from Sanaie and Attar (famous Sufi poets), and sometimes Nezaami and Khaaghaani (famous poets). Those verses were full of meaningful stories designed to teach virtue and guide people toward purification and righteousness. In those sessions they sang verses from Sanaie's book, *Elahee Naameh* (Godly Letter), and Attar's book, *Mantegho-tair* (Conference of the Birds), which added a special warmth and passion to their meetings. Rumi's love for Sanaie's poetry went back to the time when he studied with his beloved teacher, Termezi. To Rumi and

72

his followers, *Elahee Naameh* was like a holy book by which they would even sometimes swear, as at other times they would swear by the holy Koran. In this book, Sanaie, with a wonderful Sufi passion, mixed the profound parables and stories of the prophets and grand Sufi masters of the past with elegant insights. While Rumi's disciples were meeting, Rumi was still immersed in Ghazals, which were very appropriate for the sessions of Samaa and dance. The Rubaiyat (quatrains) and Ghazals initiated with Shams' name or in Shams' remembrance were mainly related to Samaa, particularly during the years that Shams and Salah-uddin were among them.

Composing Mathnavi

It has been said that one day, Rumi's followers, especially Hosam-uddin, asked Rumi if he could compose poetry in a style similar to Attar and Sanaie's poetry, which the mystics and Sufis had been reciting and reading in their congregations, so they could benefit from it and also use it as a teaching book. Rumi took out from his turban (head band) a piece of paper containing eighteen verses. Rumi then stated that he had been thinking about that himself and had written these verses for this purpose. Those eighteen verses became the beginning of the first book of *Mathnavi* as it exists today. Mathnavi is a style of poetry in the Persian language with several different themes and rhythms. Ghazal is another beautiful style of poetry, for which Hafez is especially well known. Ghazal was used by Rumi and Hafez as the means for revealing their profound life and learning experiences during their turbulent journeys on the path of love. The following are a few of those eighteen verses from the *Mathnavi* edited by Dr. Soroush, which differs in some verses from the *Mathnavi* edited by Dr. Nicholson:

(Mathnavi, Book 1, starting from Verse 1)

بشنو این نی چون شکایت می کند   از جدایی ها حکایت می کند
کز نیستان تا مرا بُبریده اند   در نفیرم مَرد و زَن نالیده اند
سینه خواهم شَرحه شَرحه از فِراق   تا بگویم شرحِ دردِ اشتیاق

Listen to this reed how it is complaining,
It is telling a tale of separations.
Since I was parted from the reed-bed,
In my lament men and women have cried.
I want my chest torn from separation,
So I may explain the pain of (love) desire.

In those eighteen verses, Rumi outlines the essence of his teaching and main points in a condensed, brief, and secretive manner. He talks about separations, insanity, inexperience, maturity, desire, love, ecstasy, and especially the reed. Later, in more than 26,000 lines of poetry in the six books of *Mathnavi*, Rumi expands and provides detailed explanations of those topics and experiences in an amazing story-telling manner. Some Rumi scholars believe that the reed in the poetry is no one but Rumi himself, who tells the most profound stories. Perhaps Rumi sees himself as a reed sitting on God's lips who has experienced the most pure, rare, and valuable visions. Indeed, it seems as if someone else is blowing into him and whatever comes out of Rumi's mouth is someone else's voice and words being channeled through him and coming out of his throat, making him sing and chant the most exquisite poetry of all time.

Rumi, at the request of Hosam-uddin and his other disciples, decided to share his magnificent visions, knowledge, experience, love, and joy with the whole world. He had tasted the magical potion of love and his body, mind, and soul were intoxicated with such an elation and bliss that he wanted to share those feelings and pleasure with others and reach the entire world. Thus, he sat like a burning fire among his students and followers, emanating light and warmth almost every night until the dawn of a new morning. How lucky and fortunate his companions were. Imagine knowing someone in whose incredible energy and wisdom you could immerse yourself, benefiting from such an immense source of love, intelligence, and insight. Rumi must have been singing new verses throughout the night and, all of a sudden, his followers looked up and it was morning again. As Rumi was in that state of euphoria, Hosam-uddin and others were writing down all of his recitations. What a great favor they have done for mankind in allowing this incredible spring of information, wisdom, and love to flow throughout time so that you and I today can drink a few sips of that incredible clear water of love, knowledge, and insight today. Rumi reveals so much fascinating information about this world and beyond through his beautiful fables and stories in verses. To appreciate and better comprehend their gathering until dawn, let us see what Rumi himself has stated through his marvelous poetry.

(Mathnavi Book 1, starting from Verse 1807)

عذر مختومی حسام الدین بخواه   صبح شد ای صبح را صبح و پناه

در صبوحی با می منصور تو   تافت نور صبح و ما از نور تو

It became dawn, oh the one that dawn is dependent upon,
Please convey apologies for the ending, oh Hosam-uddin.
Dawn's light shined and from Your light,
We are drinking the morning-wine from Your victorious wine.

(Mathnavi Book 2, Verse 1849)

جز به درد دل مجو دلخواه را   جز به شب جلوه نباشد ماه را

Only at night the moonlight can be seen,
Only with heartache you can find your heart's dream.

    It is evident from the order of the poems and stories in *Mathnavi*, that Rumi had become a spontaneous geyser of knowledge, wisdom, and love. He leapt from one story to another, without any predetermined order or premeditated arrangement. He had been transformed into a loudspeaker channeling all the immeasurable insight, awareness, and sensations transmitted through him. He passed them on to the disciples who were so enthusiastically and lovingly gathered around him, like butterflies or moths circling a blazing candle. Rumi was in such a high state of over-powering spiritual ecstasy and exultation that he was spontaneously telling stories in the form of poetry. Sometimes he jumped from one story to another without even realizing it. It is obvious that he did not plan or think of his words beforehand, but just became a free flowing fountain of love, information, and insight. The words burst through him like a volcano in which the lava fountain shoots to the air from deep within the earth, blasting to the surface with heat and energy. The bubbles are released, not based upon any prior order and arrangement, but randomly, just like Rumi's verses. It is very obvious from most of the stories and poems in the books of *Mathnavi* that this is the way these books evolved.

It is also evident that sometimes Rumi's stream of passionate poetry unexpectedly stopped. As he says himself:

(Mathnavi Book 1, Verse 131)

شرح این هجران و این خون جگر   این زمان بگذار تا وقت د گر

Explaining this despair and the bleeding heart,
Leave it now for another time.

(Mathnavi Book 2, Verse 1706)

این سخن ناقص بماند و بی قرار   دل ندارم بی دلم معذور دار

This talk was left unfinished and unsettled,
I lost heart, I am without vigor, forgive me.

At other times, when someone entered their gathering who was not worthy of hearing such valuable knowledge and wisdom, Rumi would also suddenly stop, as he states in the *Mathnavi* as follows:

(Mathnavi Book1, Verse 2385)

چون که نامحرم درآید از درم   پرده در پنهان شوند اهل حرم

When a stranger comes to my door,
The people in the harem hide behind the veil.

(Mathnavi Book 5, Verse 3938)

چون حقیقت پیش او فرج و گلوست   کم بیان کن پیش او اسرار دوست

Since the truth to him is only craving for food and lust,
Say less in front him about the secrets of our Beloved.

77

(Mathnavi Book 3, Verse 20)

تا نگویی سر سلطان را بکس   تا نریزی قند را پیش مگس

So you would not tell the secret of the King to just anyone,
So you would not pour sugar before a fly.

To a great extent, the six books of *Mathnavi* are very
much indebted to Hosam-uddin's request, persistence, and
enthusiasm. Those sessions came into existence due to Hosam-
uddin's effort, since he had become Rumi's muse and Khalifeh
(1260; 658 HG). Rumi has alluded to this throughout the
Mathnavi, as is apparent in the subsequent verses:

(Mathnavi Book 1, starting from Verse 2378)

بی کشنده خوش نمی گردد روان   این سخن شیر است در پستان جان
واعظ از مرده بود گوینده شد   مستمع چون تشنه و جوینده شد
صد زبان گردد به گفتن گنگ و لال   مستمع چون تازه آمد بی ملال
پرده در پنهان شوند اهل حرم   چون که نامحرم درآید از درم
برگشایند آن ستیران روی بند   چون در آید محرمی دور از گزند

This talk is milk in the breast of the soul,
It does not nicely flow without sucking.
When the listener became thirsty and seeking,
The speaker starts speaking even if he were dead.
When the listeners came refreshed without fatigue,
The dumb and mute find a hundred tongues to speak.
When a stranger comes to my door,
The people in the harem hide behind the veil.
But if a harmless relative comes in,
Those covered ones will lift up their veils.

As Rumi's followers also acknowledged, Hosam-uddin's
contribution would stay forever as a debt owed by the "people of
love and unity." Composing *Mathnavi* occurred during the last
fourteen years of Rumi's physical life on this earth. There was a
two-year break in the composition of *Mathnavi*, just before the
beginning of the second book, due to Hosam-uddin's wife

passing away (1262; 660 HG). Hosam-uddin had loved his wife ardently and, as a result of her death, he became extremely mournful and heartbroken, did not remarry, and did not continue the *Mathnavi* session for two years.

Rumi's younger son, Ala-uddin, died that same year at the age of thirty-six (1227-1262; 624-660 HG). Ala-uddin had become a respectable theologian and teacher but Rumi, out of sorrow, apparently did not participate in the funeral and left town. Since Sultan-Valad, who was not that close to his brother, composed some sad verses, it is clear that Rumi and his family did not take Ala-uddin's death lightly or with indifference.

During the two-year hiatus, Rumi, who had apparently recovered more quickly than Hosam-uddin from the passing of his loved ones, spent his time in the daily sessions and nightly Samaa. As usual, he composed beautiful Ghazals during his turning and euphoria. This two-year interruption is clearly indicated in the first few verses in the beginning of the second book of *Mathnavi*.

(Mathnavi Book 2, starting from Verse 1)

مهلتی بایست تا خون شیر شد   مدتی این مثنوی تاخیر شد

خون نگردد شیرشیرین خوش شنو   تا نزاید بخت تو فرزند نو

باز گردانید ز اوج آسمان   چون ضیاءالحق حسام الدین عنان

بی بهارش غنچه ها ناکفته بود   چون به معراج حقایق رفته بود

چنگ شعر مثنوی با ساز گشت   چون زدریا سوی ساحل بازگشت

This Mathnavi was delayed for a while,
An interval was necessary for the blood to transform to milk.
Until your fortune would not bear a new child,
The blood would not become sweet milk;
listen carefully.
Because the Light of God, Hosam-uddin,
drew the reins back from the zenith of heaven.
Since he had gone to the ascension of the truth,
Without his spring (presence) the buds had not bloomed.

79

When he returned from the sea to the shore,
The harp poetry of Mathnavi was attuned.

At this time, Hosam-uddin was around forty years old (1264; 662 HG), and, as indicated earlier, Rumi had officially designated him as his Khalifeh and successor. In contrast to the opposition that had arisen to Shams and Salah-uddin, all of Rumi's supporters accepted Hosam-uddin without any resistance or dissatisfaction. Not only was he a learned and knowledgeable man, but he had also spent a lot of time, energy, and money to solve the disciples' problems. Once the *Mathnavi* sessions resumed again, there were no other interruptions to its composition and dictation until the end of Rumi's life. Five other books were added to the first one. Each book was completed in around two years, despite the fact that, at the end of the second book, Hosam-uddin's short-lived illness created a brief pause. Hosam-uddin's passion and fervor for the continuation of *Mathnavi* inspired Rumi also to become very eager and excited about its completion. Whenever they found appropriate time in Samaa sessions, in the public bath, in their nightly gatherings, sitting or standing, the creation of *Mathnavi* proceeded. As is apparent at the beginning of every book, Rumi, with admiration and gratitude, made some reference to Hosam-uddin's role in the progress and extension of *Mathnavi*. Hosam-uddin's immersion in *Mathnavi*'s profound, elegant, and stunning parables and stories, which were Rumi's spiritual visions and experiences, was so intense that, once in a while during the years of its evolution, he would see in his dreams that God's prophet (Mohammad, peace and blessings be upon him) was reading *Mathnavi* with passion, satisfaction, and pride. Sometimes in a stage between wakefulness and sleep, a stage of Sufi discovery, he could see that the angels and spirits, with swords in their hands, were taking the people who opposed and rejected *Mathnavi* to hell.

The third book of *Mathnavi* was most likely started around the time that Rumi was sixty years old. Rumi's body, from continual fasting, ablutions, and Samaa, was gradually becoming exhausted and once in a while would show signs of illness, but his spirit was at the pinnacle of its strength. His supporters' enthusiasm and admiration, and particularly Hosam-uddin's love, had kept Rumi young and he would never feel too old for the passionate Ghazals and long Samaas. Even the sixth and final book of *Mathnavi*, which was written during the last two years of his life, is replete with youthful ardor and exultation. Hosam-uddin was fifty years old by the time *Mathnavi* was completed. Due to his crucial part in the *Mathnavi*, Rumi's admirers everywhere will always feel indebted to him and consider the *Mathnavi* as an "explanation of Rumi's secret."

Rumi's Exceptional Love for Hosam-uddin

In the ten-year period, prior to the start of the second book until the end of the sixth book (1264-1274; 662-672 HG), which was the last decade of Rumi's life, Hosam-uddin's efforts to look after the affairs of Rumi's followers gave Rumi the opportunity to concentrate more on his own spiritual discoveries. Rumi loved Hosam-uddin so ardently that he would not become passionate and ecstatic without his presence in any gathering. Moin-uddin Parvaaneh, who was the vizier of Kaykhosro the Third and the real power of Konya, once invited Rumi to his house with a group of prominent people. Since Hosam-uddin was out of town in his garden, Rumi remained silent despite the requests of the people at the gathering. Parvaaneh, who wisely understood Rumi's reason for silence, immediately sent someone after Hosam-uddin. When Hosam-uddin entered the gathering and was greeted warmly by Parvaaneh, Rumi became extremely joyous and loudly called Hosam-uddin his life and beloved. Then Rumi broke his silence and mesmerized the audience with his insight and wisdom. Rumi held Hosam-uddin in such high esteem that it was difficult to recognize who was the Sheikh (spiritual guide and teacher) and who was the *Moreed* (follower). When the Akhiyan group had dedicated a Khaneghah to Hosam-uddin, called Zia-uddin, Rumi accompanied the people who were taking Hosam-uddin with a special ceremony to this Khaneghah. As a sign of his deep admiration and love for Hosam-uddin, Rumi carried Hosam-uddin's prayer rug over his shoulder and walked on foot among the Akhiyans and other companions all the way to the Khaneghah.

During these times, the *Mathnavi* sessions were continually taking place at Hosam-uddin's persistence and request. Samaas were held at Hosam-uddin's house, in the school, or in the houses of the disciples or prominent people of Konya. During these gatherings, Rumi composed the most beautiful Ghazals and songs. In the daily sessions, as was customary since Salah-uddin's time, Rumi's statements and talks were written down and recorded. This collection later became the book called *Fihi-Ma-Fihi*. Hosam-uddin oversaw all the recording of Rumi's daily talks and nightly sessions. He even wrote Rumi's personal letters with his fine penmanship as Rumi dictated. Hosam-uddin loved Rumi so much that he once asked his permission to convert from Shafei Mazhab, which was his father's sect, to Hanafi Mazhab, the original sect of Rumi and his father. However, Rumi, who was concerned with "the roots of the roots of the roots of religion," did not agree to the conversion, which was related to "the branches of the branches of the branches of religion," and prevented him from this action. Like Salah-uddin, over the years Hosam-uddin had also sincerely spent all of his wealth for Rumi and his supporters. It is no wonder that Rumi compared Hosam-uddin's sacrifice to the Prophet's disciple Abu Bakr Saddigh, who spent his wealth for the holy Prophet and Islam. As a token of his appreciation, Rumi forwarded whatever gifts were sent to him to Hosam-uddin's house. As is apparent throughout *Mathnavi* and some of Rumi's other verses, during the ten years that Hosam-uddin was his Khalifeh and up until the very end of Rumi's life, Hosam-uddin was Rumi's number one and favorite Moreed. For Rumi, Hosam-uddin had become Shams' image and remembrance.

CHAPTER 7

RUMI'S BIG VENTURE

AND GAMBLE

ON

LOVE

What is Love?

What is this magical force, which is the reason for the creation of the whole universe and the essence of our being? What is this potent magical potion of love that transformed a learned, orthodox theologian into the lover of all time? What is this power we call love? Is it an electromagnetic energy and connection to the unimaginable, infinite frontier and border of beingness and beyond? What is this magical wine, which intoxicates and frees a human soul from its boundaries and connects it to a higher plane of sacred existence? Is love the only thing that can quicken the flow of the energy of one's soul or is love a reconnection to the incredible divine origin from which we came? Are we all links in an infinite chain that has no end and no beginning? Is each of us just a connection to the next link and the next and so on, or is it by reuniting with other links that we in fact have connected and become one with the rest of the universe and the incredible essence of its creation?

This amazing experience of reunification is what Rumi must have gone through when Shams linked him to his chain and brought him back to the true and majestic path of love. With this reunion, Rumi became one of the most magnificent lovers of all time. A burning fire must have been roaring deep within Rumi's soul until he met Shams, who blew away the ashes and allowed that fire to come to the surface and blaze free of any obstacle. This metamorphosis, which took place in the deepest and most secretive part of Rumi's existence, changed an incredible, rigidly educated scholar into a liberated, devoted, soaring lover, who became an inspiration for mankind.

How can anyone reach such a state of ecstasy, one in which sorrow and suffering are the same as pleasure and enjoyment? How can anyone reach a stage in which he or she can say, "I am continually at peace with the Father of the Universe and this world is like heaven in my eyes"? Can any human being rise to such an incredible elevation in his life that pain and misery have the same effect as joy and happiness? Are joy and happiness another side of pain and misery? Are madness and sanity of the same essence? Unless you experience these extreme opposite feelings and mental states, you cannot come to the realization that they are different sides of the same coin. It doesn't matter at a given moment which side of the coin is up, since they both belong to the same essence and are inseparable parts of the same reality from opposite ends. Can anyone be at his or her happiest and saddest at the same time? When sadness and happiness merge together and neutralize each other, you realize that they all converge at the same point, even if they originate from opposite ends. This point of convergence is the place of understanding the reality, which loudly and clearly affirms that nothing matters, since we are all on an incredible majestic journey toward infinity.

Is it true that when you discover that incredible magical essence of your existence buried deep down inside your soul, nothing really matters anymore? There is no hatred, there is no desire, there is no fear, and there is no hopelessness. When you are free at last from the imprisonment of your own thoughts, imagination, and doubts, a clear picture will emerge from all of those hazy and fuzzy appearances that you might have imagined or seen before. If love can make a mountain dance and the whole universe sing in an incredible and joyful song of divine unity, why are we so imprisoned by our vanity, desires, wishes, and ignorance?

Rumi took an enormous gamble on love. On the surface, he had everything to lose and almost nothing to gain. He was a well-known, respected, and prominent religious authority with his own school and many students and followers. Rumi was highly esteemed by the ruler, important people in positions of power and wealth, and other religious leaders in the region. His disciples and supporters loved and admired him. How could he choose to follow a penniless drifter, throw off his turban and robe, and dance in public? He must have realized that this behavior was political suicide, which would surely result in defaming his name, losing his societal prestige and status, and becoming the laughing stock and subject of ridicule of almost everyone in the region. Indeed, it is very difficult for any individual to ever sacrifice his good name. People are willing to lose even wealth and position to protect their good names. Shakespeare brilliantly explained this notion in Othello, when he wrote:

Good name in man and woman, dear my lord,
Is the immediate jewel of their souls:
Who steals my purse steals trash; 'tis something, nothing;
'Twas mine, 'tis his, and has been slave to thousands;
But he that filches from me my good name
Robs me of that which not enriches him
And makes me poor indeed.

(The Oxford Shakespeare, Othello, the Moore of Venice, Act 3, Scene 3, beginning from line 180)

Throughout history, willingly defaming oneself has been only the action of heroes and very extraordinary people. The first result of this venture for Rumi was, as expected, his denigration, particularly in the eyes of the conservative and influential people of his own time. Shams had shown him an amazing path through love, introducing him to the most incredible attribute of the Supreme Creator, the God of Love, which he obviously had not seen as clearly prior to his encounter with Shams. Up to this point in his life, through his studies, education, and reading of scholars such as Imam Mohammed Ghazzali, Rumi had learned to concentrate more on the fearful aspects of God and religion. However, when a tiny old man named Shams of Tabriz revealed to Rumi the more wondrous and magnificent attribute of God, the glorious Divine love, his perspective radically changed. As a result, his thoughts, attitudes, and understanding were transformed in every area, including his religious teachings. Love must have incredibly quickened the flow of his soul's energy to let him reach a high state of ecstasy and enlightenment. Through his previous rigorous and fearful way, attaining that amazing status would have possibly taken him several lifetimes.

This new perspective must have enticed him with an extraordinarily jubilant feeling and fiery desire. However, Rumi also had a lot to lose, including his prestige, title, students, school, and high regard in the eyes of the ruler and prestigious people of that region. Nevertheless, the temptation for this gamble must have been very strong. On the surface, Rumi's potential loss greatly outweighed any conceivable gain. He was risking all that he had worked so diligently to achieve in his life. Furthermore, it was not clear what he would achieve if he would win this gamble. However, I believe that in his heart, he must have realized that losing all the privileges, fame, respect, and comforts of the material life would be worth just a moment of that higher state of love and ecstasy. After all, this state of euphoria is the highest aspect of a human being's existence. The real essence of the human journey in this world is to reach that high state and the awareness that accompanies it. Therefore, Rumi decided to take this gamble. In one of his poems, he explains his circumstances most clearly and beautifully:

(Divane Shams, Rubaiyat 1891)

زاهد بودم ترانه گویم کردی
می خواره بزم و باده خویم کردی

سجاده نشین با وقاری بودم
بازیچه کودکان کویم کردی

I was devout,
you made me a poet;
You made me a tippler at the revelry,
and made me a lover of wine (of love).
I was a dignified praying man,
You made me the playmate of children in the street.

In another poem he further explains his reasons for his profound love for Shams:

89

همه را بیازمودم ز تو خوشترم نیامد
چو فرو شدم به دریا چو تو گوهرم نیامد

سر خنبها گشادم ز هزار خم چشیدم
چو شراب سرکش تو به لب وسرم نیامد

چه عجب که در دل من گل و یاسمن بخندد
که سمن بری لطیفی چو تو در برم نیامد

ز پیت مراد خود را دو سه روز ترک کردم
چه مراد ماند زان پس که میسرم نیامد

دو سه روز شاهیت را چو شدم غلام و چاکر
بجهان نماند شاهی که چو چاکرم نیامد

خردم بگفت بر پر ز مسافران گردون
چه شکسته پا نشستی که مسافرم نیامد

چو پی کبوتر دل بهوا شدم چو بازان
چه همای ماند و عنقا که برابرم نیامد

چو پرید سوی بامت ز تنم کبوتر دل
بفغان شدم چو بلبل که کبوترم نیامد

برو ای تن پریشان تو و آن دل پشیمان
که ز هر دو تا نرستم دل دیگرم نیامد

I have tried everyone,
I didn't like anyone better than you;
When I dove into the ocean,
I didn't find any pearl like you.
I opened wine barrels,
drank from one thousand barrels,

No fierce wine like yours,
was to the liking of my lips and head.
No wonder if flower and jasmine smile in my heart,
Since no delicate jasmine figure like you,
ever came into my arms.
In following you for two, three days,
I left my own desire,
What desire was left after that,
which did not become possible for me?
For two, three days,
I became the servant,
and obedient of your kingship;
There was no king in the world,
who did not become my servant.
My wisdom said to fly higher
than the voyagers of the universe;
Why are you sitting with a broken foot
that my voyager did not come?
Since my heart's dove flew
to your roof from my body,
I sang like a nightingale,
that my dove didn't come back.
Chasing my heart's dove,
I soared to the sky like eagles,
What osprey and bald eagle
could become my equal?
Go away,
my miserable body and remorseful heart;
Until I did not flee from both,
a new heart did not come to me.

It is amazing how unexpectedly life events turn out when we are fearless and courageous enough to take a great risk. How wonderfully Rumi's gamble paid off, beyond anyone's dream. However, if that gamble had not paid off for Rumi, it would not have mattered at all. Let us consider what he says himself about that gamble:

(Divane Shams, 1085)

خنک آن قمار بازی که بباخت آن چه بود ش
بنماند هیچش الا هوس قمار دیگر

Lucky that gambler who lost whatever he had,
Nothing was left for him
but a desire for one more gamble.

Due to Shams' influence, Rumi reached the highest peak in his love journey in a short time (around two years). If Rumi had not met Shams, he might not have been able to climb to that exhilarating height even by the end of his life. All of a sudden, Divine Destiny had placed in his path an old vagabond who showed him a different path, perspective, and vision of a new reality about life's journey, the universe, and especially its Supreme Creator, the God of Love and the reason for the creation of the universe itself - glorious love. How fortunate and lucky for him! He had the courage to take on such a huge venture and proceed with no fear of losing whatever he had gained during his entire life up to that point. In one of the poems in *Divane Shams*, Rumi vividly explains, from his own mind and thoughts, that astonishing interaction and dialogue between the two of them and his stunning transformation.

(Divane Shams, 1393)

مرده بدم زنده شدم گریه بدم خنده شدم
دولت عشق آمدومن دولت پاینده شدم

دیدهَ سیر است مرا جان دلیر است مرا
زهرهَ شیر است مرا زُهره تابنده شدم

گفت که دیوانه نه ای لایق این خانه نه ای
رفتم و دیوانه شدم سلسله بندنده شدم

گفت که سرمست نه ای رو که از این دست نه ای
رفتم و سرمست شدم و ز طرب آکنده شدم

گفت که تو کشته‌نه‌ای در طرب آغشته‌نه‌ای
پیش رخ زنده کنش کشته و افکنده شدم

گفت که تو زیرککی مست خیالی و شکی
گول شدم هول شدم وز همه برکنده شدم

گفت که تو شمع شدی قبله این جمع شدی
جمع نیم شمع نیم دود پراکنده شدم

گفت که شیخی و سری پیش رو و راهبری
شیخ نیم پیش نیم امر ترا بنده شدم

گفت که با بال و پری من پر و بالت ندهم
در هوس بال و پرش بی پر پرکنده شدم

گفت مرا دولت نو راه مرو رنجه مشو
زانکه من از لطف و کرم سوی تو آینده شدم

گفت مرا عشق کهن از بر ما نقل مکن
گفتم آری نکنم ساکن و باشنده شدم

چشمهٔ خورشید تویی سایه گه بید منم
چونکه زدی بر سر من پست و گدازنده شدم

تابش جان یافت دلم واشد و بشکافت دلم
اطلس نو بافت دلم دشمن این ژنده شدم

صورت جان وقت سحر لاف همی زد ز بطر
بنده و خربنده بدم شاه و خداونده شدم

شکر کند خاک دژم از فلک و چرخ بخم
کز نظر و گردش او نور پذیرنده شدم

شکر کند چرخ فلک از مَلِک و مُلک و مَلَک
کز کرم و بخشش او روشن بخشنده شدم

93

شكر كند عارف حق كز همه بردیم سبق

بر زبر هفت طبق اختر رخشنده شدم

از تو ای شهره قمر در من و در خود بنگر

کز اثر خندهٔ تو گلشن خندنده شدم

باش چو شطرنج روان خامش و خود جمله زبان

کز رخ آن شاه جهان فرخ و فرخنده شدم

I was dead,
I became alive,
I was tears,
I became laughter;
The majesty of love came,
and I became an everlasting majesty myself.
My eyes are full (have seen everything),
I have a brave soul;
I have the guts of a lion,
I became the shining Venus.
He (Shams) told me, "You are not insane,
you are not worthy of this house;"
I became insane and I linked with his chain.
He said, "You are not drunken, go,
you are not from this type;"
I went and became drunken and full of joy.
He said, "You are not dead (selfless),
you are not mixed with joy;"
In front of his life-giving face I fell and I died.
He said, "You are cunning,
intoxicated with dreams and doubts;"
I became a fool
I became fearful
I became detached from everyone.
He said, "You became the candle,
the Ghebleh (pole) for this gathering;"
I am not (in) a group,
I am not a candle,
I became evaporated smoke.

94

He said, "You are the Sheikh and the head,
you are the leader and the guide;"
I am not the Sheikh,
I am not the guide,
I am the servant of your command.
He said, "You have wings and feathers,
I will not give you (any more) wings and feathers;"
In desire of his wings and feathers,
I became featherless and wingless (without wings).
The new fortune told me, "Do not walk and exhaust yourself,
because from love and mercy I am coming toward you."
He (Shams) said to me, "Do not tell us from the old love."
I said, "Yes, I will not;"
I became inactive and motionless.
You are the spring of sunlight,
I am the shadow of the weeping willow;
Since you touched my head,
I became modest and burning with desire.
My heart received the light of life,
my heart opened up and bloomed;
My heart wove a new silk,
I became the enemy of the old one.
The soul's face at the time of dawn,
bragged from euphoria;
I was a servant and a slave,
I became a king and a supreme being.
The depressed soil would thank
the galaxies and the universe,
That from his attention and rotation,
I became light absorbing.
The universe thanks
the King of the Universe and the angel,
That from his generosity and mercy,
I became illuminated and merciful.
The mystic would thank God,
that we surpassed everyone;
Above the seven skies,
I became the shining star.

I am yours, oh beloved of the whole world,
look at me and look at yourself,
From your smile,
I became a laughing flower garden.
Be like a flowing chess game,
silent and expressive,
From the image of the King of the World,
I became fortunate and auspicious.

Shams showed Rumi an extraordinary and demanding path. Only a very few fortunate individuals possess the required valor, willingness to sacrifice, longing, strength, and right combination of characteristics to explore such an unknown territory. In the following verses, Rumi describes the burden of love from its very beginning and the people who are drawn to it:

(Mathnavi, Book 3, Verse 4752)

تا گریزد آنک بیرونی بود   عشق از اوّل چرا خونی بود

Why is (the path of) love bloody from the beginning?
So whoever is not worthy of it would flee from it.

(Mathnavi, Book 5, Verse 1165)

در حریف بی وفا می ننگرد   عشق چون واقی است وافی می‌خرد

Since love is loyal, it only desires the loyal,
Love does not even glance at a disloyal companion.

In another poem, Rumi further explains the effect and consequences of love on him:

(Mathnavi, Book 6, starting from Verse 902)

چون شکرشیرین شدم از شور عشق   عشق قهار است و من مقهور عشق
من چه دانم که کجا خواهم فتاد   برگ کاهم پیش تو ای تند باد

نه به زیر آرام دارم نه زبر او همی گرداندم بر گرد سر
یک دمی بالا و یک دم پست عشق گربه در انبانم اندر دست عشق
بر قضای عشق دل بنهاده اند عاشقان در سیل تند افتاده اند
ریشخند سبلت خود می‌کند با قضا هر کو قراری می نهد

Love is the subduer,
and I am subdued by love;
From love's passion,
I became sweet like sugar.
Oh, fierce wind (of love),
in front of you I am only a straw;
What do I know,
where I will fall?
Love is spinning me around its head,
I have serenity neither above nor below.
In love's hand I am a cat caught in a sack,
From love, one moment up, one moment down.
The lovers have fallen in a severe flood,
They have put their hearts into love's destiny.
Whoever makes a covenant with destiny,
He is mocking his own moustache (himself).

When Rumi started to whirl and sing, the most beautiful poetry of all time began to flow from his lips. The poetry came to him with no effort, as he became an instrument, allowing the messages to pass through him for the people of all generations. It must have been an incredible journey and transformation, coming from rigidity and being constrained by the stringent rules and regulations of theology, to become a liberated, carefree spirit to whom no one's opinion and scorn held any value or worth. He must have become so drunk with that potion of love that Shams poured into his soul, existence, and essence that nothing mattered anymore.

When Rumi threw off his turban and robe and started Samaa in the streets, bazaar, and in other public places, everyone must have been shocked and amazed by his transformation. As he said himself in his verses, he became the laughing stock of the town. At first, people must have looked at him and thought that he had lost his mind. They must have thought that the Sheikh had gone crazy and the old drifter Shams had put an incredible spell or played an astonishing trick on Rumi and he was under an unbelievable trance or hypnotic effect. As the rumors started to circulate, Shams was accused of trickery and sorcery, which possibly resulted in the termination of his physical life. However, for Rumi the gamble paid off beyond his wildest dreams and imagination. He abandoned public admiration and a well-known, secure position in society for an unknown future that only in his heart he believed was right. For the first time, he must have understood that the passage through the heart is much quicker than the passage through the mind. Through love Rumi could soar miraculously and quickly to the skies and connect to that inconceivable source of power of the whole universe, the God of Love.

Other roads might never have taken him that quickly and that far. If he had followed the path of mind and intellect, who knows where he would have ended up and how long it would have taken him. In only about two years, Shams had influenced Rumi's life so unbelievably that it might have often seemed like a dream even to him. Of course, no one can really tell what went through his mind except by reading his beautiful poetry and trying to understand his state of mind and emotions.

Love and Fear

Rumi was reaching for the God of love, instead of the God of fear. He was loving God, instead of fearing God. Love and fear are two different powerful emotions. They both have very strong effects on people and play incredible roles in their lives. Isn't it true that we are mostly ruled by our fears and loves? Which is stronger and more effective? Which is more forceful and makes us move faster and become more conscientious? Love and fear – we do many things because of fear and we do even more because of love. If you place fear and love on two sides of a scale and try to add up all the different weights that are carried with each one, you are forced to conclude that the side of love must have been much heavier for Rumi and he must have felt that in his soul and heart. Otherwise, why would he have so enthusiastically thrown off his turban and robe, started to dance in public, and compose some of the most beautiful verses of all time while doing his Samaa? This new discovery about love and its magical effects had indeed elevated him incredibly quickly to the peak of a mountaintop of euphoria and enlightenment, which he had never reached before. He explains this feeling as follows:

(Mathnavi Book 1, Verse 1570)

بُوالعَجَب من عاشق این هردو ضد   عاشقم بر قهر و بر لطفش بجد

I am truly in love with God's mercy and wrath,
What a wonder, I am in love with these two opposites.

(Mathnavi Book 4, Verse 3262)

این جهان چون جنت هستم در نظر   من که صلحم دائما با این پدر

I am always at peace with the Father (of the universe),
This world is like paradise in my eyes.

باده غمگینان خورند وما ز می خوشدل تریم

رو به محبوسان غم ده ساقیا افیون خویش

خون غم بر ما حلال وخون ما بر غم حرام

هر غمی کوگرد ما گردید شد در خون خویش

The sorrowful drink wine
and we are more jubilant than wine,
Oh cupbearer (wine giver),
go and give your opiate (wine) to the prisoners of sorrow.

In other verses he declares:

(Mathnavi Book 5, starting from Verse 2184)

جمله قربانند   اندر کیش عشق   ترس موئی نیست اندر پیش عشق

وصف بنده مبتلای فرج و جوف   عشق وصف ایزد است اما که خوف

خوف نبودوصف یزدان ای عزیز   پس محبت وصف حق دان عشق نیز

از فراز عرش تا تحت الثری   عشق را پانصد پراست و هرپری

عاشقان پران تر از برق و هوا   زاهد با ترس می تازد به پا

کآسمان را فرش سازد دردعشق   کی رسند این خایفان برگرد عشق

Fear is not even (as thin as) a hair in the sight of love,
Everything is expendable in the path of love.
Love is the description of the Beloved (Almighty),
But fear is the description of the servant (man)
afflicted by lust and emptiness.
Therefore, love and devotion is the depiction of God,
Fear is not the depiction of God, my dear.
Love has five hundred feathers,
And each feather ascends from heaven to eternity.
The fearful devout runs on foot,
The lovers leap faster than lightning and the wind.
How would the fearful even catch the dust of love?
The passion of love makes the sky its carpet.

(Divane Shams, 396)

در ره معشـوق مـا ترسندگان را کار نیست

جمله شاهانند آنجا بردگان را بار نیست

In the path of our Beloved,
fearful have no business,
There, all are kings,
slaves have no place.

Think for a moment how remarkable this state of mind must be for a human being. You reach such a point of ecstasy and exultation in your life journey that good news and bad news have the same effect on you. Wrath and mercy are the same. Happiness and sorrow are the same. What an incredible state of mind this must be, when nothing really matters. You are so incredibly content with your journey on the majestic path of love and discovery that just being on that journey and path is all that matters. Nothing else has any value or any merit in your eyes. You are consumed only by the love of One, as Rumi says:

(Divane Shams, Nicholson's Selected Poems, Page 125)

مکانم لا مکان باشد نشانم بی نشان باشد

نه تن باشد نه جان باشد که من از جان جانانم

دویی از خود بدر کردم یکی دیدم دو عالم را

یکی جویم یکی دانم یکی بینم یکی خوانم

اگر در عمر خود روزی دمی بی او برآوردم

از آن روز و از آن ساعت ز عمر خود پشیمانم

My home is beyond any place,
My place is beyond any address,
It's not the body,
it's not the soul.
I am from the dearest of the dears,
The soul of the Supreme Creator.

I rid myself from duality
and see both worlds as one,
I seek one (God),
I know one,
I see one,
I call one.
If in my entire life,
I spent one breath without my Beloved,
I am regretful about that hour and day of my life.

Can you imagine yourself at some point in your life reaching a state of such ecstasy that nothing really matters? At that point, you are so content and blissful that nothing can affect you. Your core center is absolutely under your own control and no one's actions or reactions can change your actions and direction. You are finally the master of yourself, no longer a slave to anyone or anything, including your own temptations, desires, and passions. You have only one passion and one desire – to reunite with your Beloved, the Supreme Master Creator of love and the universe. Let us consider what Rumi says in another poem in *Divane Shams*:

(Excerpts from Divane Shams, Shafiee Kad Kani, Page 580)

ما در ره عشق تو اسیران بلاییم
بر ما نظری کن که درین مُلک غریبیم
زُهدی نه که در کنج مناجات نشینیم
نه اهل صلاحیم و نه مستانه خراییم
حلّاج وَشانیم که از دار نترسیم
ترسیدن ما چو که هم از بیم بلا بود
مارابتوسرّیست که کس محرم آن نیست
مارا نه غم دوزخ و نه حرص بهشت است
بر رحمت خود بین و مبین بر گنه ما
دریاب دل شمس خدا مفخر تبریز

کس نیست چنین عاشق بیچاره که ماییم
برما کرمی کن که درین شهر گداییم
وجدی نه که بر گِردِ خرابات برآییم
اینجا نه و آنجا نه چه قومیم و کجاییم
مجنون صفتانیم که در عشق خداییم
اکنون ز چه ترسیم که در عین بلاییم
گر سَر برود سِرِّ تو با کس نگشاییم
بردار ز رخ پرده که مشتاق لقاییم
ما غرق گناه از سَر تا ناخن پاییم
رحم آر که ما سوختهٔ داغ خداییم

In the path of Your love,
we are the prisoners of tragedy;
No one is in love as hopelessly as we are.
Look at us,
we are strangers in this land;
Have mercy for us,
that we are beggars in this town.
No virtue to sit in the praying corner,
No fervor to turn to the tavern.
We are neither the pious kind,
nor the drunken one;
Neither from here,
nor from there,
from what tribe,
or from where are we?
We, like Hal-laj (renowned Sufi master who was hung for
saying "I am God"),
are not afraid of hanging,
We, like Majnoon (Arabian Romeo),
are insanely in love with God's love.
Since our fear was worrying about tragedy,
Why should we be afraid now,
that we are in the midst of tragedy?
We are privileged to share a secret of yours,
of which no one is worthy;
If we lose our heads,
we will not reveal your secret to anyone.
We have no worry for hell,
and no desire for heaven;
Unveil Your face since we are longing for the reunion.
Look at Your mercy and not at our sins,
We are drowned in sin from head to toe (nail).
Oh God, heal the heart of Shams, the honor of Tabriz,
Have mercy that we are burned by God's separation.

What an incredible crossing – coming from fear to love. If you really reflect on your own life or that of someone you know, you realize that people do much more for love than they do for fear. For example, if you fear your boss, you will try to do what is required to meet the boss' expectations. Then imagine you love your boss. You will go out of your way, work overtime, and stay in the office day and night without expectations, just because you have that warm feeling for your boss. On the contrary, if you fear your boss, you do only what is required of you. This is not true in the case of love. You sacrifice your time and energy without expectations of return. Hence the splendid feeling of love is much stronger and more powerful than fear.

I believe this is what happened to Rumi. Before meeting Shams, he was an orthodox scholar and theologian, full of God's fear, who endeavored to obey all the rules and regulations of religion in order to be a good person and behave appropriately. However, when he met Shams, the transformation that took place was phenomenal, beyond any explanation. As Rumi says in the following verses:

(Mathnavi, Book 1, starting from Verse 112)

هر چه گویم عشق را شرح و بیان   چون به عشق آیم خجل باشم از آن

گر چه تفسیر زبان روشن گر است   لیک عشق بی زبان روشن تر است

چون قلم اندر نوشتن می شتافت   چون به عشق آمد قلم برخود شکافت

عقل در شرحش چو خر درگل بخفت   شرح عشق و عاشقی هم عشق گفت

عاشقی پیداست از زاری دل   نیست بیماری چو بیماری دل

Whatever I say about love,
When love comes I am ashamed of my explanation.
Even though the explanation of the tongue sheds some light,
Love without explanation is much clearer.
When it came to love,
My pen that was hurrying in writing, broke from its glory.
In explaining love,
intellect was caught like a donkey in the mud,
Only love could explain the story of love and the lovers.
Being in love is apparent from the heart's cry,
There is no illness like the illness of the heart.

(Mathnavi Book 2, Verse 1770)

عاشقان را ملت و مذهب خداست   ملت عشق از همه دین ها جداست

Love's nationality is separate from all other religions,
The lover's religion and nationality is the Beloved (God).

(Mathnavi, Book 1, Verse 110)

عشق اصطرلاب اسرار خداست   علت عاشق ز علت ها جداست

The lover's cause is separate from all other causes,
Love is the astrolabe of God's mysteries.

In this new state of contentment, Rumi had reached a point of euphoria where nothing mattered to him anymore. He was in love with the Divine Creator and the whole universe. The world was heaven to him. To him, wrath or mercy was the same – bitter or sweet was the same. Can you imagine how intoxicated he must have been with the wine of love that nothing mattered anymore? This new feeling must have elevated and propelled him extremely high in order to tap into the higher planes of existence and frequencies that allowed him to experience the most astonishing visions about our world, the universe, and higher states of existence and reality. He must have reached an extraordinary level of understanding. From this new high elevation and vantage point, he could see and understand everything in a much better light and perspective. He could comprehend the makeup of this world and higher worlds, and understand why this world is the way it is.

Nothing could disturb his peace and solitude. He was now a solid island of stability and serenity in the middle of the ocean of life's uncertainty and unpredictable waters. Now he was so ecstatic and in love that he wanted to share his feelings and wisdom with the whole world as he went into those wonderful states of euphoria and drunkenness. As Rumi states in *Divane Shams*:

(Excerpts from Divane Shams, Shafiee Kad Kani, Page 578)

تو مپندار که من شعر بخود میگویم
تا که بیدارم و هشیار یکی دم نزنم

Do not think that I compose poetry by myself,
When I am aware and conscious,
I do not say a word.

(Divane Shams, 1611)

مکن ایدوست غریم سر سودای تو دارم
من و بالای مناره که تمنای تو دارم
زتو سرمست وخمارم خبر ازخویش ندارم
سر خود نیز نخارم که تقاضای تو دارم
دل من روشن و مقبل زچه شد با توبگویم
که در این آینهٔ دل رخ زیبای تو دارم

مکن ای دوست ملامت بنگر روز قیامت
همه موجم همه جوشم در دریای تو دارم

هله ای گنبد گردون بشنو قصه‌ام اکنون
که چو تو همزه ماهم بر و پهنای تو دارم
بر دربان تو آیم ندهد راه و براند
خبرش نیست که پنهان چه تماشای تو دارم
ز درم راه نباشد ز سر بام و دریچه
سَتَرَاللهُ عَلَینا چه علالای تو دارم

هله زین پس نخروشم نکنم فتنه نجوشم
بدلم حکم کی دارد دل گویای تو دارم

Oh my beloved, don't make me a stranger,
I have your desire in my head;
I am on the top of the minaret (world),
but still longing for you.

106

Because of you I am drunken and intoxicated,
I am not conscious of myself,
I do not even scratch my head,
since I have only your desire.
I tell you how my heart
became illuminated and happy (lucky),
Because in the mirror of my heart,
I have your beautiful image.
Oh, my beloved, do not scold me,
Look at the Day of Justice.
I am all waves,
I am all excited,
I am desirous of your ocean,
Hail, oh spinning universe,
now listen to my saga.
Since, like you, my companion is the moon,
I have your size and magnitude.
I come to your doorman,
he does not let me in and chases me;
He doesn't know how I secretly watch you.
If there is no path through the door,
I come from the roof and windows. ...
From now on I will not cry out,
I will not make mischief,
I will not be enraged,
Whose directive is in my heart?
My heart expresses only you.

SECTION II:

RUMI'S DISCOVERIES

ON

THE MAJESTIC PATH

OF

LOVE

CHAPTER 1

THE UNIVERSE,

SCIENCE, TECHNOLOGY,

AND

REALITY

Around 750 years ago, through his secret eye, higher senses, and spiritual visions, Rumi discovered and understood the mechanism and structure of the universe, its realities and its mysteries. Through his beautiful poetry, he explains and describes the incredible issues that scientists have recently discovered through science with laboratory experiments, mathematical calculations, and sophisticated tools and devices. No wonder Rumi states so clearly:

(Mathnavi Book 2, starting from Verse 3551)

حس دل را هر دو عالم منظر است   مر دلم را پنج حس دیگر است

برتو شب بر من همان شب چاشتگاه   تو ز ضعف خود مکن در من نگاه

My heart has five other senses,
The heart senses observe both worlds.
Do not look at me from your weakness,
To you it is the night and that night to me is the morning.

In another poem he declares:

(Mathnavi Book 5, starting from Verse 3935)

غالب آمد چشم سر حجت نمود   چشم سر با چشم سر در جنگ بود

مر عصا را چشم موسی چوب دید
چشم غیبی افعی و آشوب دید

پیش چشم غیب نوری بد پدید   چشم موسی دست خود را دست دید

The secret eye was in conflict with the physical eye,
The secret eye triumphed and showed the way.
Moses' (physical) eye saw the staff as a wood,
His secret eye saw it as a serpent and trouble.
Moses' (physical) eye saw his hand as a hand,
To his secret eye it appeared as light.

In *Divane Shams*, Rumi also reminds us:

(Divane Shams, 1390)

ما را بچشم سَرمبین ما را بچشم سِرّ ببین
آنجا بیا ما را ببین کانجا سبکبار آمدم

Don't look at us with the eyes in your head,
Look at us with your secret eye,
Come there and see us,
That I came there free of burden.

Rumi with his secret eye and higher senses saw both worlds - the present one and the higher one. Through his incredible visions and discoveries, he described phenomena such as the force of gravity, nuclear physics and explosions, the sun's light, the spinning galaxies, the Earth's rotation that brings day and night, matter and antimatter, electromagnetic frequencies in relation to the higher senses, the illusion of our reality, and the true reality. Rumi explains that we give existence to our bodies, and they do not have an existence of their own. He teaches us why our world is always so turbulent and unstable and there is no peace on this earth. Rumi reveals many other fascinating scientific facts and phenomena that we have discovered only recently due to advances in science and technology. In the following chapters, I will provide some examples of Rumi's ingenious discoveries and accurate descriptions of those magnificent wonders.

The Creation of the Universe

(Mathnavi Book 6, starting from Verse 3134)

عقل می‌کارید اندر آب و طین   ما کجا بودیم کان دیان دین

وین بساط خاک را می‌گسترید   چون همی کرد از عدم گردون پدید

و ز طبایع قفل با مفتاح‌ها   ز اختران می ساخت او مصباح‌ها

مضمر این سقف کرد و این فراش   ای بسا بنیادها پنهان و فاش

Where were we when the Judge of Judgment Day,
Was planting intelligence in water and clay (creatures)?
When God created the universe from nothingness,
And was spreading the carpet of the earth,
From stars was making lamps (lights),
And from nature locks with keys (problems with solutions).
God enclosed in this ceiling (sky) and this carpet (earth),
Many foundations (details) concealed and revealed.

(Mathnavi Book 5, starting from Verse 1024)

که بر آرد ز و عطاها دم به دم   پس خزانه صنع حق باشد عدم

که بر آرد فرع بی اصل و سند   مبدع آمد حق و مبدع آن بود

هست را بنمود بر شکل عدم   نیست را بنمود هست و محتشم

Therefore, nothingness is the treasure of God's creation,
From which God brings out gifts every moment.
God is the originator and the originator is that,
Who creates branches without roots and foundation.
God made nothingness to appear existent and magnificent,
God made the existent to appear in the form of nothingness.

If you think for a moment about the grandness of the universe, you will realize what a spectacular, awesome feat occurred at the beginning and is still continuing. Just imagine before the creation of time, over twelve billion years ago, there was nothing but a seething mass of energy smaller than an atom.

114

From this almost nothing point, the universe expanded a hundred trillion trillion trillion times!

According to Professor Steven Hawking[2], world-renowned physicist from Cambridge University, the universe started with a big bang from a single point called singularity. At the point of singularity, gravity was infinitely strong, space and time as we know them did not exist, and there was no matter. This almost nothing point, called singularity, expanded to become this glorious, incredible, and endless universe which is still expanding. Dr. Hawking believes that the universe eventually may contract and become that singularity again. Professor Albert Einstein's famous discovery $E = MC^2$ showed that energy and mass are interchangeable, and allowed us to understand that the pure energy of the universe could be converted into matter. Professor Einstein also stated that God does not play dice with the universe. I believe this means that the universe's grand architecture is so perfectly designed that nothing is left to chance or random events. In reality, we are living on a tiny planet, in the grand, boundless cosmos. As Dr. Hawking explains, the universe has no beginning and ending in time and has no edge. Therefore, it is truly infinite. What an incredible phenomenon – coming from nothingness to infinity and probably from infinity to nothingness again. From the very new findings, we also know that there are black holes in the center of galaxies. Some are very active and continue to absorb massive amounts of materials from the galaxies back into the black holes. No wonder Rumi stated in the above verses, "*God made nothingness to appear existent and magnificent, God made the existent to appear in the form of nothingness.*"

The above review of recent scientific research confirms Rumi's ingenious and incredible visions and discoveries as described in the previous verses. It is extraordinary that more than 750 years ago, Rumi through his higher senses and insight, without the benefit of advanced scientific tools, was able to comprehend and explain such a magnificent phenomenon as the creation of the universe out of nothingness.

The Creation of Heaven and Earth

(Mathnavi Book 1, starting from Verse 2386)

درميان بس نارونورافراخته است   حق زمين وآسمان برساخته است
آسمان را مسكن افلاكيان   اين زمين را از براى خاكيان
مشترى هر مكان پيدا بود   مرد سفلى دشمن بالا بود

God has created the Earth and the sky (Asemaan),
In their midst (God) has lit many a fire and light.
This Earth for the Earthly beings,
The sky (Asemaan) the home for the celestial.
The man from below is the enemy of above,
The seeker of each place is known (by their action).

We now know that the birth of stars involves nuclear reactions which produce light, fire, and energy. It is fascinating that Rumi so long ago talks about fires and lights in the midst of space.

(Mathnavi Book 3, starting from Verse 2905)

خالق آب و تراب و خاكيان   خالق افلاك او و افلاكيان
آب و گل را تيره رويى ونما   آسمان را داد دوران و صفا
كى تواند آب وگل صفوت خريد   كى تواند آسمان دردى گزيد
كى كهى گردد به جهدى چون كهى   قسمتى كرده است هريك را رهى

The Creator of the universe and celestial beings,
The Creator of water and soil and the Earthly beings,
Gave the sky (Asemaan) circular motion and purity,
(Gave a mixture of) water and soil
dark appearance and growth.
How can the sky choose turbidity?
How can (a mixture of) water and soil acquire purity?
(God) has divinely destined for each one a path,
How can a mountain become a straw with any effort?

I should note that *Asemaan*, the word for sky in Farsi, means beyond the planet Earth, outer space. It is interesting that Rumi in the above verses describes the circular motion in the sky (Asemaan). Nowadays we know that the galaxies have spinning motions and there is continuous movement throughout the universe.

Why God Created the Universe

In *Divane Shams*, Rumi conveys God's purpose for the creation of the universe:

(Divane Shams, 3426)

می گفت با حق مصطفی چون بی نیازی زما
حکمت چه بود آخر بگو در خلقت هر دو سرا

حق گفت ای جان جهان گنجی بدم اندر نهان
می خواستم پیدا شود آن گنج احسان و عطا

The Prophet (Mohammad, peace and blessings be upon him)
was saying to God,
"Since you are needless of us,
Say at last,
what was the reason in creating both worlds?"
God said, oh soul of the world,
I was a hidden treasure,
I wanted that treasure of grace and mercy to be found.

In *Mathnavi*, Rumi further expounds upon God's reason for the magnificent creation in the following verses:

(Mathnavi Book 2, starting from Verse 2635)

گفت پیغمبر که حق فرموده است   قصد من از از خلق احسان بوده است
آفریدم تا ز من سودی کنند   تا ز شهدم دست آلودی کنند

The holy Prophet said that God has stated,
My intention for the creation has been love (mercy).
I created so they would benefit from me,
And infuse their hand with my honey.

(Mathnavi Book 2, Verse 1756)

من نکردم امر تا سودی کنم   بلکه تا بر بندگان جودی کنم

I didn't create to profit,
But to be generous to the creatures.

(Mathnavi Book 2, Verse 2631)

از برای لطف عالم را بساخت   ذره ها را آفتاب او نواخت

For love God created the universe,
Every particle benefited from God's Sun of mercy.

Everything in the Universe Praises God

As I explained earlier in the introduction, it has taken me close to 20 years to understand some lines of Rumi's poetry during times of meditation and higher spiritual awareness and consciousness. The following verses are excellent illustrations of the depth of Rumi's poetry and his profound discoveries about the mysteries of creation. What we all may consider as inanimate and not living, with no function, motion, and sound, in reality, in higher states of frequencies and consciousness, are in fact not what they appear to be. We may realize that they are far from being silent and lifeless. From my own personal experiences during my wonderful times of meditation, sometimes I could clearly hear that everything around me was praising the Supreme Creator in a beautiful, harmonious, and synchronous manner. I also recall that a Sufi Master once stated that the sounds in the universe kept him awake at night.

(Mathnavi Book 3, starting from Verse 463)

باز از پستی سوی بالا شدیم   کز جهان زنده ز اول آمدیم
ناطقان کآنا الیه راجعون   جمله اجزا در تحرک در سکون
غلغلی افکند اندر آسمان   ذکر و تسبیحات اجزای نهان

From the beginning we have come from the living world,
Once again from this low end (world),
we soared to the high end (world).
All the particles in motion or motionless,
Are proclaiming, "Verily we are returning to God."
The worship and the praises of the hidden particles,
Have filled the skies with an uproar.

(Mathnavi Book 3, starting from Verse 1020)

محرم جان جمادان چون شوید   چون شما سوی جمادی می روید
غلغل اجزای عالم بشنوید   از جمادی عالم جان ها روید

120

فاش تسبیح جمادات آید   وسوسه تأویل ها نربایدت

چون ندارد جان تو قندیل ها   بهر بینش کرده ای تأویل ها

که غرض تسبیح ظاهر کی بود   دعوی دیدن خیال غی بود

Since you are going toward inanimateness (materialism),
How can you become intimate
with the life of inanimate beings?
From inanimateness go toward the world of spirits,
And hear the sound of the particles of the world.
The glorification of God
by inanimate beings will become apparent to you,
The temptation of (false) interpretations
does not misguide you.
Since your life has no lamp (light) for seeing,
You have made (false) interpretations.
How can the visible glorification (of God) be the intention?
The claim of seeing is the flawed fantasy.

Sunlight, Spinning Galaxies, and the Force of Gravity

A few decades ago, Edwin Hubble cataloged the galaxies and described their shapes and motions, including our Milky Way galaxy. We also know that our sun's light, heat, and energy are the result of continuous nuclear fusion, which transforms four hydrogen atoms to one atom of helium on the sun's surface. Let's see how Rumi has referred to these issues in the third book of *Mathnavi* around 750 years ago:

(Mathnavi Book 3, starting from Verse 4)

نه از فتیل و پنبه و روغن بود   این چراغ شمس کو روشن بود

نه از طناب و استنی قایم بود   سقف گردون کو چنین دایم بود

The burning light of the sun,
Is not from burning oil and the wick.
Our spinning galaxy, which is so continuous,
Is not structured on columns and fastened by wires.

We know that gravity is the main force in the motion and arrangement of our universe, the Milky Way galaxy, the solar system, and the planet Earth. According to the famous story, in the seventeenth century Sir Isaac Newton discovered the force of gravity by observing an apple falling from a tree. The following verses express Rumi's insight about gravity, long before Newton:

(Mathnavi Book 3, Verse 4402)

با توام چون آهن و آهن ربا   آسمان گوید زمین را مرحبا

The sky hails the Earth,
I am with you as the iron is with the magnet.

(Mathnavi Book 1, starting from Verse 2487)

چون حکیمک اعتقادی کرده است   که آسمان بیضه زمین چون زرده است

گفت سایل چون بماند این خاکدان   در میان این محیط آسمان

همچو قندیلی معلق در   نه به اسفل می رود نه بر علا

آن حکیمش گفت کز جذب سما   از جهات شش بماند اندر هوا

چون ز مغناطیس قبه ریخته   در میان ماند آهنی آویخته

بلکه دفعش می کند از شش جهات   زان بماند اندر میان عاصفات

The humble sage has believed that
The sky is an egg and the Earth its yolk.
The inquisitor asked how this Earth remains,
In the midst of the surrounding sky -
Like a lamp suspended in the air,
Neither moving to the bottom nor to the top.
The sage told him, "From the attraction of the sky,
from six directions it remains in the air.
(The sky is) like a vault molded of lodestone,
It (the Earth) is suspended in the middle like a piece of iron.
Because it (the sky) is repelling the Earth from six directions,
Therefore, it (the Earth) remains suspended
in the midst of the fierce storm."

Rumi compares the Earth to a yolk and the surrounding sky to an egg. He clearly explains that the force of gravity from all six directions is required to keep the Earth suspended and in equilibrium. Rumi further uses an interesting analogy in which he compares the sky to a vault made of lodestone (magnetized piece of magnetite) which can keep a piece of iron in the middle of it in a state of balanced equilibrium. Rumi expresses the above concept very clearly and centuries before Copernicus (1473-1543), William Gilbert (1546-1603), Galileo (1564-1642), Kepler (1571-1630), and Newton (1642-1727).

123

The Earth's Rotation

Long before Galileo (1564-1642), Rumi (1207-1273) alludes, in the next few verses, to the Earth's rotation, which is the reason for night and day to appear one after the other.

(Mathnavi Book 3, starting from Verse 4416)

مختلف در صورت اما اتفاق   شب چنین با روز اندر اعتناق

لیک هر دو یک حقیقت می تنند   روز و شب ظاهر دو ضد و دشمنند

از پی تکمیل و فعل کار خویش   هر یکی خواهان دگر را همچو خویش

Night and day embrace each other,
Different at surface, but united (in essence).
Day and night at the surface are opposites and enemies,
But they both reveal the same truth.
Every one of them desiring the other, like its own,
For the completion of its own task and work.

(Divane Shams, 1407)

چون رخ آفتاب شد دور ز دیدهٔ زمین

جامه سیاه میکند شب زفراق لاجرم

خور چه بصبح سر زند جامه سپید میکند

ای رخت آفتاب جان دور مشو ز محضرم

...

When the face of the sun
became distant from the eyes of the Earth,
The night from separation wears black clothes consequently.
When the sun rises in the morning,
it (the Earth) wears the white clothes.
Oh your face, the sun of life,
do not go away from my presence.

It is obvious that Rumi is stating that day and night, despite the fact that they seem like opposites, actually come one after another in a circular fashion to complete each other's work and when one finishes, the other starts. This is an indication that he talks about the Earth's rotation resulting in days and nights.

Nuclear Explosion

In the first, second, third, and sixth books of *Mathnavi*, Rumi explicitly asserts that inside of particles there is an awesome hidden power that can be released. At the present time we refer to this phenomenon as a nuclear reaction and explosion.

(Mathnavi Book 6, starting from Verse 4580)

آفتابی در یکی ذره نهان   ناگهان آن ذره بگشاید دهان

ذره ذره گردد افلاک و زمین   پیش آن خورشید چو جست از کمین

Inside of each particle there is a hidden sun,
Suddenly that particle opens its mouth.
The galaxies and the Earth become shattered,
In front of that sun when it comes out of hiding.

(Mathnavi Book 1, Verse 2502)

اینت خورشیدی نهان در ذرّه   شیر نر در پوستین برّه

There is a sun hidden in a particle,
The male lion in lamb's clothing.

(Mathnavi Book 2, starting from Verse 1395)

دُر چه دریا نهان در قطرهٔ   آفتابی مخفی اندر ذرّهٔ

آفتابی خویش را ذرّه نمود   و اندک اندک روی خود را برگشود

جملهٔ ذرّات در وی محو شد   عالم از وی مست گشت و صحو شد

What a pearl, a sea hidden in a drop,
A sun concealed in a particle.
A sun portrayed itself as a particle,
And little by little uncovered its face.

All particles disappeared in it,
The world became intoxicated and sober from it.

(Mathnavi Book 3, Verse 1983)

تا ببینم قُلزُمی در قطرهٔ   آفتابی   دَرج   اندر   ذرّه

I see an ocean in a drop,
A sun contained in a particle.

The Higher Senses

Rumi brilliantly reveals the existence of our higher senses in addition to our five physical senses. He openly proclaims:

(Mathnavi Book 2, starting from Verse 47)

آن چو زرّ سرخ و این حسها چو مس   پنج حسی هست جز این پنج حس

حس مس را چون حس زر کی خرند   اندر آن بازار کایشان ماهرند

حس جان از آفتابی می چرد   حس ابدان قوت ظلمت می خورد

حس دُر پاشت سوی مشرق روان   حس خفاشت سوی مغرب دوان

> *There are five other (spiritual) senses*
> *besides our five (bodily) senses.*
> *Those (spiritual senses) are like red (pure) gold;*
> *these (bodily) senses are like copper.*
> *In the (higher) world that they (extra senses) are skillful,*
> *The copper (bodily) senses are not valued*
> *like the gold senses.*
> *The bodily senses are consuming the food of darkness,*
> *The spiritual senses are nurturing from the sun (sunlight).*
> *Your bat-like (bodily) senses are running*
> *toward the west (sunset),*
> *Your pearl-disseminating (spiritual) senses*
> *are flowing toward the east (sunrise).*

(Mathnavi, Book 2, starting from Verse 65)

پس بدیدی گاو و خر الله را   گر بدیدی حس حیوان شاه را

جز حس حیوان ز بیرون هوا   گر نبودی حس دیگر مر تو را

کی به حس مشترک محرم شدی   پس بنی آدم مکرم کی بُدی

> *If the animal sense could see the King (God),*
> *then the ox and the donkey would see Allah (God).*
> *If you had no other senses,*

besides and outside of the animal senses,
When could you be the honorable son of Adam?
When could you become privileged to the common sense?

For the reader to better understand what Rumi describes here, in the next segment I provide some scientific background in order to clarify Rumi's fascinating discovery about our higher senses.

The Spectrum of Frequencies

Dr. Stuart Bowyer, Professor Emeritus of Astronomy at the University of California at Berkeley, states that the whole spectrum of electromagnetic radiation goes from gamma rays, very high energy electromagnetic radiation, X-rays, ultraviolet, visible (red to violet), infrared, micro waves, and finally to radio waves. Furthermore, the whole band carries information and each band tells us something different.

The world that we call our own for the time being is the planet Earth. For now, we are stationed on this beautiful planet with blue skies and waters and different colorful creatures that are a feast to one's eyes. This is our visible world in the red to violet frequency domain. Sight is one of our most important senses. We can see colors, shapes, patterns, flowers, trees, oceans, and the sky. We can see things through a magnificent vision system. Our eyes work like a camera. The lens focuses images onto the retina, a light sensitive tissue spread like a film on the back of the eye. Light stimulates groups of specialized nerve cells called retinal ganglions. Retinal ganglions send the information via electrical signals to the optic nerves, which connect the eyes to the brain. In the occipital cortex, the vision center of the brain, the picture is developed. Scientifically speaking, we really don't see only with our eyes. What we call vision is really the picture assembled in our brain through a complicated process. We call that picture our eyesight. In fact, our eyes are really two radio telescopic antennas that receive electromagnetic waves traveling in the universe. The eyes receive frequencies of different ranges, but only have sensitivity for the limited range (band) of red to violet frequencies. The retina cells in our eyes can only distinguish the visible light frequencies between red and violet. The extent of frequencies could be infinite in the universe. Therefore, what we call our visible world is really the small realm of red to violet frequencies, which is a minute bandwidth compared with the rest. We cannot see all the other things that are not in our range of sight frequency.

Our reality is the verity of our sensors. What is real to most of us is what we can recognize with our sensory organs. Basically, our understanding of the world around us is really the perception of our sensors and our brains' interpretation and nothing else. However, as human beings, we are also equipped with higher frequency sensors. I believe that at different frequency levels there are different physical matters and beings with building blocks that are in accordance with each specific range of frequency or vibration. I will explain this later.

Wherever you are, there are several worlds or levels of realities existing simultaneously at the same location. Imagine if a snake and a honeybee are present with you at this moment. They would see things very differently from the way you see them. The snake's vision system operates in infrared, while the bee's system operates in ultraviolet frequencies. So, in reality, your view of the environment depends on the type of vision system with which you are equipped and the operational range of your visual equipment. Sometimes, it is possible to enhance our innate equipment with other tools. For example, infrared goggles enable us to see in the dark. In summary, what we see is not the reality, but only the interpretations of our mind and brain via our vision system.

When we look up in the sky at night, we are only seeing a very tiny part of what exists. For over thirty years, astronomers have realized that we actually do not know the composition of 90 percent of the universe. In fact, most of the universe has been referred to as the dark matter mystery, since it does not seem to give off light and is not optically visible. The only proof of the existence of this hidden 90 percent is the gravitational tug that it exerts, preventing galaxies from completely flying apart.

According to astrophysicist Dr. Vera Rubin, it's evident from the movement of stars in galaxies that the stars are being accelerated by an enormous amount of matter that we can't see, which is aptly called dark or black matter. Dark matter, unlike ordinary matter that emits or reflects light, is entirely invisible. However, judging from its effects, this exotic stealth-like matter is far more pervasive than common visible matter. Thus it is likely that most of the universe is constituted of a form of matter that is not the kind we see, taste, feel, or of which we are made. There is a kind of a ghostly background of particles to which we are not sensitive that constitutes about 90 percent of the universe. It is astounding that, for centuries, all our studies of the universe have actually overlooked 90 percent of it! Recently, physicists discovered ghostly particles, called neutrinos, but they may account for as little as one percent of the universe's mass. A team of U.S. and Australian astronomers has been investigating Massive Compact Halo Objects (MACHOs), dark star-sized lumps, hypothesized to be brown dwarf stars or black holes, which may make up half of the dark matter.

Dr. Brian Greene, Professor of Physics and Mathematics at Columbia University, in a recent interview explained that there is something in and around our Milky Way galaxy that is actually ten times larger than our galaxy. It is extraordinary to contemplate something so large that could be around us and yet be invisible. One theory proposes that there are particles around us called WIMPs (Weakly Interacting Massive Particles). Dr. Greene described these particles as ghostlike since everything, even a planet, can pass right through them with no effect. However, a WIMP, unlike a ghost who is weightless, weighs roughly between 10 and 500 times the weight of a single proton. This may not seem like much, but billions and billions of trillions could weigh enough to be the missing matter of the universe. Recently, scientists have actually found preliminary evidence of the existence of WIMPS.

In the very near future, supersensitive telescopes will be able to resolve more of the mysteries of the universe. At this point, we do not know exactly what created the black matter and the void in the universe. Instruments such as the new telescope Chandra, which was sent out of our atmosphere with a scope in the X-ray bandwidth, and NASA's Extreme Ultraviolet Explorer (EUVE) satellite should enable us to obtain a better picture of our universe and increase our understanding of dark matter, WIMPS, MACHOs, black holes, and energies.[3]

As I mentioned earlier, even at a physical and atomic level, there are several worlds within each other. I believe that your present existence in a particular physical world is related to your present vibrational frequency level at the moment. Thus, there are different stages of existence and different vibrational levels. On our present world on the planet Earth, we are in the vibrational level that is commonly known to us as our physical world. After we leave this world and our physical bodies, conditional on the energy of our souls (our electromagnetic energy), we will be at different vibrational or frequency levels. You could think of ghosts as beings (souls) at different vibrational levels or stages of existence. When we leave our bodies after our physical deaths, depending on our energy, we can ascend to higher vibrational worlds or frequencies to find our new place until we travel to the next higher one. Thus, our souls go through different stages of being based upon our level of energy, which is directly related to the degree of our enlightenment and evolvement. To give you a simple example to illustrate this concept, think of a glass full of clear water. If you add some red color to the water, the water becomes red. If you then add some yellow color, the water becomes a mixture of red and yellow everywhere. If you add more colors, the color of the water becomes a combination of all the added colors. Even though you see a different color as the final result, at the same time, every color that you added is present simultaneously in that mixture. Another example illustrating this concept is to imagine filling a room with different types of gases. Every gas is present at the same time in every part of the room. In the same way, you can think of the different existences and physical matters being present everywhere at the same time at different vibrational frequencies. Our normal matter is made up of the atoms we know from the periodic tables of elements and other matter in higher vibrational frequencies are presently known to us as WIMPs.

The Divine Creator of the Universe, the God of Love, has equipped us with higher senses so we can relate to other parallel existing worlds. Rumi clearly states that we all have higher senses that we can realize by following special (mystical) paths

133

and practices. Each of us was born with these higher senses and it is not difficult to recognize and take advantage of them. Consequently, our higher senses could be very useful for other worlds and different worlds of frequencies such as the ultraviolet and beyond. But how can we obtain control of these higher senses?

Rumi, in continuation of the previous poems in *Mathnavi*, teaches us how to proceed in order to attain these higher senses.

(Mathnavi Book 2, starting from Verse 69)

گر تو کوری نیست بر اعمی حرج   ور نه رو کالصبر مفتاح الفرج

پرده های دیده را داروی صبر   هم بسوزد هم بسازد شرح صدر

آینه دل چون شود صافی و پاک   نقش ها بینی برون از آب و خاک

هم ببینی نقش و هم نقاش را   فرش دولت را و هم فرّاش را

If you are blind (spiritually),
there is no fault upon you;
Otherwise, go and be patient,
that patience is the key to the victory (opening).
The medicine of patience will burn the veil over your eyes,
It will also open your heart.
When the mirror of the heart becomes clear and pure,
You will see images beyond the water and soil (the Earth).
You will see not only the image,
but the image-maker,
Not only the carpet,
but the carpet layer.

By patience, Rumi here means striving for perfection by purifying our souls and hearts so the mirror of our hearts can reflect God's light. What a true metaphor! If a mirror is dirty and full of dust, it will not reflect any light. If you clean that mirror it will reflect light to dazzle your eyes. Thus, Rumi makes a very interesting analogy between the mirror and your heart, which is the gateway to the higher spiritual worlds.

Light and Color

(Mathnavi Book 1, starting from Verse 1121)

کی ببینی سرخ و زرد و فور را   تا نبینی پیش از این سه نور را

لیک چون در رنگ گم شد هوش تو   شد ز نور آن رنگ‌ها روپوش تو

چون که شب آن رنگ ها مستور بود   پس بدیدی دید رنگ از نور بود

نیست دید رنگ بی نور برون   همچنین رنگ خیال اندرون

این برون از آفتاب و از سها   و اندرون از عکس انوار علا

نور نور چشم خود نور دل است   نور چشم از نور دل ها حاصل است

باز نور نور دل نور خداست   کاو ز نور عقل و حس پاک و جداست

شب نبد نور و ندیدی رنگ‌ها   پس به ضد نور پیدا شد تو را

دیدن نور است آنگه دید رنگ   و این به ضد نور دانی بی درنگ

رنج و غم را حق پی آن آفرید   تا بدین ضد خوش دلی آید پدید

پس نهانی‌ها به ضد پیدا شود   چون که حق را نیست ضد پنهان بود

که نظر بر نور بود آنگه به رنگ   ضد به ضد پیدا بود چون روم و زنگ

چون به ضد نور دانستی تو نور   ضد ضد را می نماید در صدور

نور حق را نیست ضدی در وجود   تا به ضد او را توان پیدا نمود

How will you see red, green, and russet,
Unless you see the light, before seeing these three (colors)?
But since your mind was lost in the color,
Those colors became your veil from the light.
Those colors were hidden at night,
Then you saw that vision was from the light.
There is no vision of color without the external light,
Similarly the color of inner dreams.
This external (light) is from the sun and star,
The inner (light) is from the reflection
of the beams of (Divine) glory.
The glow of the eye's light is the light of the heart,
The eye's light is the consequence of the heart's light.
Again, the light of the heart's light is God's light,
Which is pure and separate
from the light of intellect and sense.

135

At night there was no light, so you didn't see the color,
Therefore, the opposite of light manifested light to you .
Seeing the light is before seeing the color,
And this you know immediately
by the opposite of light (darkness).
God created pain and sorrow,
So happiness would be known from this opposite.
From the opposites, hidden things are manifested,
Since God has no opposite, God is hidden.
The intention was light, then color,
The opposite is revealed by its opposite like (the skin color of)
Romans and Ethiopians (white and black).
Therefore, from the light's opposite you knew the light,
The opposite reveals the opposite
in the process of coming forth.
God's light has no opposite in existence,
So you cannot find God from God's opposite.

The True Reality and the Perception of Reality

Persian mystics have stated that there are three kinds of certainties:

1. The certainty of science (علم‌اليقين), which is reached by gathering evidence and reasoning.

2. The certainty of seeing (عين‌اليقين), which is reached by directly seeing and observing something.

3. The certainty of God (حقّ‌اليقين), which is the complete real truth, known by the Almighty.

Rumi conveys his concept of reality in the following verses:

(Mathnavi Book 3, starting from Verse 4725)

تا ز هستان پرده‌ها برداشتی	کاشکی هستی زبانی داشتی
پرده دیگر بر او بستی بدان	هرچه گویی ای دم هستی از آن
خون به خون شستن محال است و محال	آفت ادراک آن قال است و حال

I wish that every being had a tongue,
So it would unveil the cover from its existence.
Whatever you say, oh living breath, about that (being),
You are only covering it with another veil.
A description is detrimental to true understanding,
As washing blood with blood is impossible, is impossible.

In the above verses, Rumi teaches us that the reality of any being or object is not necessarily our perception of the reality of that thing. Instead, our perception is individually tailored to our existence based upon our sensory organs and our interpretation of the sensory inputs, as explained previously in scientific terms. Therefore, by describing something, we are actually covering its truth and its entirety by looking at it from our own idiosyncratic angle. If the reality of an object or being could express and reveal its own truth, it would be very different from our perception. For example, when you look at a human body, you can view it as a beautiful work of art. However, in reality that body is 99 percent void or empty space. Of course, our perception also has a direct relationship to the limitations of our sensory organs in terms of the range of frequencies. To give you a simple example, let us look around our environment. Is reality what we actually see with our eyes and brain? Isn't this reality simply our perception of things or, as I explained earlier, just the interpretation of the pictures formed in our brain through our vision system? Would a snake or a honeybee see a rose the way we see and understand it? Since their vision systems operate in different ranges of frequencies the answer should be negative.

Another good example of the limitations of our powers of perception and interpretation is to ask ourselves if wine makes us drunk or we make the wine drunk. If you pour wine over wood, stone, or any other object, does anything happen? Is it our special makeup that produces drunkenness? Rumi's belief is found in the subsequent verses:

(Mathnavi Book 1, starting from Verse 1812)

قالب از ما هست شد نی ما ازو   باده از ما مست شد نی ما ازو

خانه خانه کرده قالب را چو موم   ما چو زنبوریم و قالب ها چو موم

The wine became drunken from us,
not us from the wine;
The body came to existence because of us,
not us from the body.
We are like the (honey) bees
and our bodies (are) like the honeycombs (waxes),
(God) Has made the body cell by cell like the honeycomb.

It is important to understand that the reason for breaking out of the false reality is to become one with the universe and return to the essence of your being. Then you unite with that essence, which is the actual reality. In this way you become a part of the true reality and truly understand the reality itself, not the perception of the reality.

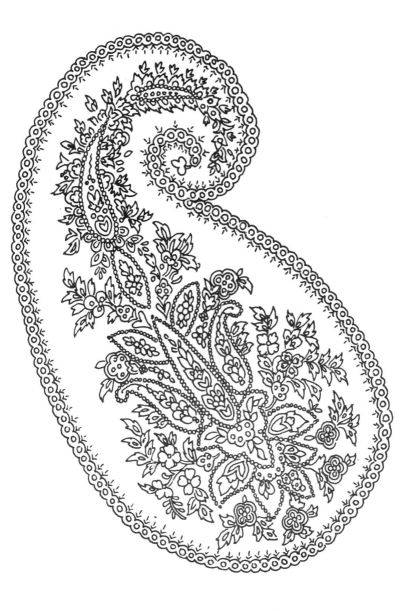

Our Contradictory and Turbulent World and Its Makeup and the Hegelian Dialectic

I have always thought that God has given us such a beautiful world. Our Supreme Maker has granted us an incredible and beautiful planet, a real jewel in the solar system and the Milky Way galaxy. Therefore, one of the most difficult concepts to understand about our world is the existence of violence, prejudice, corruption, hunger, despair, diseases, suffering, and unhappiness. What is the reason for all of the hostility, killing, injustice, misery, pain, and hunger? Why do all these negative forces exist when it would have been so easy for the Master Creator to make a perfect world with complete peace and harmony on our planet Earth? Wouldn't it be wonderful to live in a world full of love, justice, peace, and happiness, free of any disease, starvation, or wrongdoing? Why didn't the God of Love and Mercy make our world like that? We all know that for the Supreme Power it would have been effortless to make this world the opposite of how it is today. When you look at any society, country, or part of this world, you see corruption, under-the-table connections, injustice, nepotism, narcissism, and other evil actions and forces at work. Why is this? We cannot answer this question. Instead, we should really acknowledge that we do not have an adequate or complete understanding of why the world is the way it is. In *Mathnavi*, Rumi explains this in a profound, logical, and comprehensive manner.

(Mathnavi Book 6, starting from Verse 36)

ذره با ذره چون دین با کافری	این جهان جنگست کل چون بنگری
زین تخالف آن تخالف را بدان	جنگ فعلی هست از جنگ نهان
در میان جزوها حربی است هول	جنگ طبعی جنگ فعلی جنگ قول
در عناصر در نگر تا حل شود	این جهان زین جنگ قایم می بود
لاجرم ما جنگی ایم از ضرّ و سود	پس بنای خلق بر اضداد بود
هر یکی با هم مخالف در اثر	هست احوالم خلاف همدگر
با دگر کس سازگاری چون کنم	چون که هر دم راه خود را می زنم

هر یکی با دیگری در جنگ و کین   موج لشگرهای احوالم ببین

پس چه مشغولی به جنگ دیگران   می نگر در خود چنین جنگ گران

در جهان صلح یگرنگت بَرَد   تا مگر زین جنگ حقت واَخرد

زآن که آن ترکیب از اضداد نیست   آن جهان جز باقی و آباد نیست

چون نباشد ضد نبود جز بقا   این تفانی از ضد آید ضد را

که نباشد شمس و ضدش زمهریر   نفی ضد کرد از بهشت آن بی نظیر

صلح ها باشد اصول جنگ ها   هست بی رنگی اصول رنگها

وصل باشد اصل هر هجر و فراق   آن جهان اصل است این پُر غم وثاق

This world is a big war if you look at its totality,
Particle, with particle, like the believer with
the nonbeliever (as religion with infidelity).
The present war is from the hidden war,
From this animosity, learn about that animosity.
The war of nature,
the war of action,
the war of words,
Among the particles is a terrible war.
This world is maintained by this war,
Look at the elements to solve the puzzle.
Therefore, creation is based upon opposites,
Consequently we are a war of loss and profit.
My states of mind are mutually opposed,
Each one is mutually opposite in its effect.
Since at every moment I am in a struggle with myself,
How can I be in harmony with someone else?
Look at yourself and see this intense war,
Then why are you involved with others' wars?
Unless God will redeem you from this war,
and take you to the one-colored world of peace,
The higher world is everlasting and flourishing,
since its composition is not from contraries.
This reciprocal destruction comes about
from the opposition of contraries,
Since there is no opposition,
there is nothing but everlastingness.
The unique Almighty eliminated
the contradictions from paradise,

In which there is no sun (heat),
nor its opposite, severe cold.
Colorlessness is the origin of colors,
Peace is the origin of war.
That (higher) world is the origin,
and this one is a sorrowful prison,
Union is the origin of every severance and separation.

It is fascinating that these contradictions are also true at the quantum physics level. We know from the makeup of our physical world that there are matter and antimatter, positron and electron, positive energy and negative energy, and light and darkness. It should be very obvious that what is known in the Western world as the Hegelian dialectic, that synthesis is the result of thesis and antithesis, is clearly and explicitly described in the above verses. Rumi summarizes this concept by saying that the Supreme Maker has created this world, the world of contradictions, with every particle opposing another particle. It is apparent from the above verses that since this world is a summation of contradictions, it will not be everlasting and will be destroyed at the end. On the contrary, the higher world, which God created out of harmony and peace and not contradictions, will be the everlasting world.

In another poem, Rumi further explains that the dispute in the world has been continual and will last until the end of the world.

(Mathnavi Book 5, starting from Verse 3214)

همچنین بحث است تا حشر بشر   در میان جبری و اهل قدر

گر فرو ماندی ز دفع خصم خویش   مذهب ایشان بر افتادی ز پیش

چون که مقضی بُد دوام این روش   می دهدشان از دلایل پرورش

تا نگردد ملزم از اشکال خصم   تا بود محجوب از اقبال خصم

تا که این هفتاد و دو ملت مدام   در جهان ماند الی یوم القیام

Similarly, there is a debate until the Resurrection of mankind,
Between the necessitarians (fatalists)

and partisans of (absolute) free will.
If the disputant of either party
has been incapable of refuting his adversary,
Their (respective) doctrines would have vanished.
Since the continuation of that debate was divinely destined,
God feeds them both with reasons.
So he (disputant) may not be silenced
by his adversary's objection,
And he may not see his adversary's success.
Hence these seventy-two sects (ideologies) continually,
Will stay in the world till the Day of Judgment.

Rumi also teaches that the ugliness in this world does not reflect negatively on its Supreme Creator:

(Mathnavi Book 3, starting from Verse 1372)

زشتی‌خط زشتی نقاش نیست   بلکه از وی زشت را بنمودنی ا ست

قوّت نقاش باشد آنکه او   هم تواند زشت کردن هم نکو

The ugliness of a painting is not the ugliness of the painter,
But it is up to him to portray the ugliness.
The power of the painter is the ability
to paint ugliness and beauty.

The reason for the creation of ugliness is to have a contrast to beauty, so that each can be recognized separately by its differences. In general, Rumi explains throughout *Mathnavi* that everything is known accurately because of its opposite. Following are some verses to demonstrate this important concept:

(Mathnavi Book 2, Verse 3383)

زآن که هر چیزی به ضد پیدا شود   بر سپیدی آن سیه رسوا شود

Because everything is known by its opposite,
Upon whiteness the black is conspicuous.

(Mathnavi Book 5, Verse 599)

چون ببیند زخم بشناسد نواخت   جز به ضد ضد را همی نتوان شناخت

Without contrary its contrary is not known,
When one suffers a blow
then one will know (the value of) kindness.

(Mathnavi Book 6, Verse 2152)

وآن شه بی مثل را ضدی نبود   بی ز ضدی ضد را نتوان نمود

Nothing can be shown without its opposite,
That incomparable King (God) has no opposite.

(Mathnavi Book 6, starting from Verse 2157)

ضد نور پاک او قابیل شد   همچنان دور دوم هابیل شد
تا به نمرود آمد اندر دور دور   همچنان این دو عَلَم از عدل و جور
وآن دو لشکر کین گذار و جنگ جو   ضد ابراهیم گشت و خصم او

Similarly in the second period,
Cain became the opposite of the pure light of Abel.
Likewise the two banners of justice and injustice,
Were passed on period after period until Nimrod.
He became the opposite and enemy of Abraham,
And those two armies were revengeful and sought war.

(Mathnavi Book 6, Verse 2162)

تا به فرعون و به موسی شفیق   دور دور و قرن قرن این دو قرین

Generation after generation,
century after century,

144

these two opposites,
(Continued) till Pharaoh and (Holy) Moses.

(Mathnavi Book 3, starting from Verse 3762)

غم چو آیینه است پیش مجتهد   کاندر این ضد می نماید روی ضد
بعد ضد رنج آن ضد دگر   رو دهد یعنی گشاد و کرّ و فرّ

Sorrow is like a mirror in front of the learned one,
Inside this (mirror),
opposite portrays the face of opposite.
After the opposite, pain, the other opposite (happiness),
Shows its face, revealing openness, glory, and triumph.

The Origin Of Music and the Reason We Love It

Rumi reveals the origin of music and the reason we all love music, regardless of our background, in the following:

(Mathnavi Book 6, Verse 703)

مطرب آغازید پیش ُترک مست   در حجاب نغمه اسرارَاَلَست

The entertainer started in front of the drunken king,
Behind the cover of music the secret of the Alast.

What Rumi refers to as the *Alast* is a verse in the holy Koran, explaining that the Supreme Creator gathered all the creatures and asked them to acknowledge that He is their Lord, and all the creatures did so. Next is the translation of the verse:

Koran [7:172]: Recall that your Lord summoned all the descendants of Adam, and had them bear witness for themselves: "Am I not your Lord?" They all said, "Yes. We bear witness." Thus, you cannot say on the Day of Resurrection, "We were not aware of this."

In the above poetry Rumi refers to that day of gathering as referenced in the Koran. Rumi believes on that day, we were all in heaven in front of the Divine Creator. The wonderful memory of being in the presence of our Beloved in paradise, along with the music and melodies we heard there, is buried deep in our subconscious. Every time we hear music somehow we are all reminded subconsciously of that incredible, idyllic, and blissful memory and, therefore, we all love music regardless of race, nationality, religion, or any other similar distinction. Since music reminds us of our separation and also of the earlier union, music is indeed the language of the soul. Thus, music touches us in places where words cannot even come close. Rumi explains this concept further in the subsequent poem:

146

لیک بُد مقصودش از بانگ رباب   همچو مشتاقان خیال آن‌خطاب

ناله سُرنا و تهدید دُهل   چیزکی ماند به آن ناقُور کل

پس حکیمان گفته‌اند این لحن‌ها   از دَوار چرخ بگرفتیم ما

بانگ‌گردش‌های چرخ است‌این‌که خلق   می نوازندش به تنبور و به حلق

مؤمنان گویند که آثار بهشت   نغز گردانید هر آواز زشت

ما همه اجزای آدم بوده‌ایم   در بهشت آن لحن‌ها بشنوده‌ایم

گرچه بر ما ریخت آب و گِل شَکی   یادمان آمد از آنها چیزکی

لیک چون آمیخت با خاک کَرَب   کی‌دهند این زیر و این‌بم آن‌طرب

پس غذای عاشقان آمد سماع   که در او باشد خیال اجتماع

قُوَّتی گیرد خیالات ضمیر   بلکه صورت گردد از بانگ و صفیر

آتش عشق از نواها گشت تیز   آنچنان که آتش آن جُوز ریز

But God's intention from the sound of the rebeck (pear-shaped stringed musical instrument),
It is like for the lovers (of God),
the fantasy of that (God's) allocution (formal speech).
The crying of the clarion and the menace of the drum,
Somewhat resembled that grand (universal) trumpet.
Therefore, the sages have said these melodies,
We have taken from the spinning (sound) of galaxies.
It is the sound of the spinning galaxies that people
Play with the pandore (ancient musical instrument similar to a guitar) and sing with the throat.
The righteous believers say that the influence of heaven
Made every unpleasant sound to be beautiful.
We all have been parts of Adam,
In paradise we have heard those melodies.
Even though water and soil (mixed with our soul)
poured a doubt,
We still remember something of those (melodies).
But since it (melody) was mixed with depressed soil,
How should this treble and bass give (us) the same delight?
Therefore, Samaa became the food for lovers,
Therein lies the dream of reunion.

The mental fantasies gather strength,
although they become images from tune and sound,
The love fire became inflamed from the melodies...

According to the holy Koran, the grand (universal) trumpet is the trumpet that the Angel Israfil plays to announce the Day of the Resurrection.

Koran [18:99]: On that day We shall leave them to surge like waves on one another: the trumpet will be blown, and We shall collect them all together...

The following verse is found in the New Testament, Book of Revelation:

Revelation [11:15]: Then the seventh angel blew his trumpet, and there were loud voices in heaven, saying, "The kingdom of the world has become the kingdom of our Lord...

Rumi states that when our soul was mixed with our body, which is naturally made mostly of water and other elements from the soil, our memories were somehow blocked and doubt fell upon us because of that lack of complete recollection. However, we still remember something from the prior memories of our soul, which heard those beautiful melodies and tunes in paradise when we were all parts of Adam. Another amazing piece of information that Rumi discloses is that the motion of the universe creates music and melodies that we try to imitate with our musical instruments and our voices in song.

The Continual Renewal of
Our Bodies and World

(Mathnavi Book 1, starting from Verse 1144)

بی خبر از نو شدن اندر بقا   هر نفس نو می‌شود دنیا و ما

مستمری می‌نماید در جسد   عمر همچون جُوی نو نو می‌رسد

آن ز تیزی مستمر شکل آمدست

چون شرر کش تیز جنبانی بدست

With every breath, we and the world become anew,
Unaware of being renewed while it remains (the same).
Life arrives like a stream anew,
In the body it seems continuous.
From its quickness, it appears continuous…

It is fascinating that around 750 years ago with limited available knowledge and information regarding the human body and the universe, Rumi recognized such a scientific phenomenon through his spiritual insight and experiences. We now know that the human body is truly an ocean of intelligence, energy, and information. The body is continually revitalizing itself in every moment of its existence.

In a normal breath of fresh air, we breathe in a tremendous number of molecules from the atmosphere. Professor C. Donald Ahrens[4], a geophysicist from the California Institute of Technology, has stated that an average-size breath of air is about a liter. In a liter of fresh air near sea level there are roughly 10^{22} air molecules. Therefore, with every breath we breathe in 10^{22} air molecules.

We can appreciate how large this number is when we compare it to the number of stars in the universe. Some of these inhaled molecules become parts of our body and some are exhaled. According to Dr. Hamid Rasoul, Professor of Physics and Space Sciences and Director of Geospace Physics Laboratory at the Florida Institute of Technology, astronomers have estimated that there are about 100 billion (10^{11}) stars in an average-size galaxy and that there may be as many as 10^{11} galaxies in the universe. To determine the total number of stars in the universe, we multiply the number of stars in a galaxy by the total number of galaxies and obtain:

$$10^{11} \times 10^{11} \sim 10^{22} \text{ stars in the universe.}$$

Therefore, each breath of fresh air contains about as many molecules as there are stars in the known universe. In the entire atmosphere there are nearly 10^{44} molecules. Since the number 10^{44} is 10^{22} squared, as $10^{22} \times 10^{22} = 10^{44}$ molecules in the atmosphere, we conclude that there are about 10^{22} breaths of air in the entire atmosphere. In other words, there are as many molecules in a single breath as there are breaths in the atmosphere. If the Earth's population was 10^{22} (the current population is 6×10^{9}), and all of us breathed at the same time, we could suck all the molecules in the atmosphere into our lungs!

Thus, we all literally share the same atmosphere, as with every breath, we take in approximately 10^{22} molecules from all over the universe, and breathe out approximately 10^{22} molecules into the turbulent universe. If we wait a long time, those molecules will eventually become thoroughly mixed with all of the other air molecules. If none of the molecules were consumed in other processes, eventually there would be a molecule from that single breath in every breath that is out there. Therefore, considering the many breaths people exhale in their lifetimes, it is possible that in our lungs are molecules that were once in the lungs of people who lived hundreds or even thousands of years ago. It is fascinating to contemplate this miraculous sharing of our atmosphere and universe.

As Rumi so beautifully and accurately states in the above verses, our bodies are indeed perpetually revitalizing themselves. It is a well-known medical fact that even our blood is continually revitalized as our red blood cells are replaced every twenty-eight days and our blood platelets are replaced every eight to ten days. According to Dr. Deepak Chopra[5], in any given three weeks a quadrillion atoms that have circulated through our bodies have also circulated through the body of every other living species on our planet. In addition, Dr. Chopra states that it is estimated at the atomic level that we actually replace 98 percent of our bodies' atoms in less than a year, making new skin once a month, a new liver every six weeks, a new stomach lining every four days, and a new skeleton every three months.

CHAPTER 2

LIFE JOURNEY

AND

HUMAN NATURE

Human's Journey from Solid to Infinity

Rumi ingeniously describes the cycle of life, its process, and evolution in the subsequent verses:

(Mathnavi Book 3, starting from Verse 3900)

و ز نما مُردم به حیوان سر زدم   از جمادی مُردم و نامی شدم

پس‌چه ترسم‌کی ز مُردن‌کم شدم   مُردم از حیوانی و آدم شدم

تا بر آرم از ملایک پَرّ و سر   حمله دیگر بمیرم از بشر

آنچه اندر وهم ناید آن شوم   بار دیگر از مَلَک قربان شوم

I died from solid and became plant,
From plant I was transformed to animal.
From animal I died and became a human,
Then why should I be afraid of death?
I never became less from death.
Next I die from human,
and soar to become an angel,
I soar again from an angel,
and become something that you cannot even imagine.

(Divane Shams, Nicholson's Selected Poems, Page 125)

مکانم لا مکان باشد   نشانم بی نشان باشد

نه تن باشد نه جان باشد که من از جان‌جانانم

My home is beyond any place,
My place is beyond any address.
It's not the body,
It's not the soul.
I am from the dearest of the dears,
The soul of the Supreme Creator.

روزها فکر من این است و همه شب سخنم
که چرا غافل از احوال دل خویشتنم

از کجا آمده ام آمدنم بهر چه بود
به کجا میروم آخر ننمائی وطنم

مانده ام سخت عجب کز چه سبب ساخت مرا
یا چه بوده است مراد وی از این ساختنم

جان که از عالم علویست یقین میدانم
رخت خود باز بر آنم که همانجا فکنم

مرغ باغ ملکوتم نیم از عالم خاک
دو سه روزی قفسی ساخته اند از بدنم

خنک آن روز که پرواز کنم تا بر دوست
بهوای سر کویش پر و بالی بزنم

کیست در گوش که او میشنود آوازم
یا کدامست سخن میکند اندر دهنم

کیست در دیده که از دیده برون مینگرد
یا چه جانست نگوئی که منش پیرهنم

تا بتحقیق مرا منزل و ره ننمائی
یکدم آرام نگیرم نفسی دم نزنم

می وصلم بچشان تا در زندان ابد
از سر عربده مستانه بهم در شکنم

من بخود نامدم اینجا که بخود بازروم
آنکه آورد مرا باز برد تا وطنم

تو مپندار که من شعر بخود میگویم
تا که هشیارم و بیدار یکی دم نزنم
شمس تبریز اگر روی بمن بنمائی
والله این قالب مردار بهم در شکنم

These are my daily thoughts and nightly cries,
Why am I so oblivious to my own state of heart?
Where have I come from,
what have I come for?
To where am I going,
won't you show me my real home?
I am very much puzzled for what reason God created me,
Or what has been God's intention for my creation.
The spirit is from the higher world,
I know that for certain,
I intend to hang my clothes there again.
I am the bird from the garden of paradise,
and not from this world of dust,
For a few days I have been caged in this body.
How wonderful the day that I fly toward my Beloved;
I spread my wings in desire of His Kingdom.
Who is in my ears that hears my cry?
Who is putting words in my mouth?
Who is in my eyes that looks out of my eyes?
What is the spirit that I am its attire?
Till you show me the path and home for certain,
I will not be calm for a breath,
I will not talk for a moment.
Let me taste the wine of your reunion,
So I smash the prison door of eternity with drunken uproar.
I have not come here by myself to go back by myself,
The one who has brought me here,
will take me home again.
Do not think that I compose poetry by myself,
When I am aware and conscious,
I do not say a word.
Oh Shams of Tabriz, if you show your face to me,
I swear to God that I will break out of this dead body.

156

The cycle of life that is briefly described in the above verses is scientifically accurate. We all know that vegetation and plants grow using nutrients in the soil. At the atomic level, we realize that all the atoms in vegetation and plants come from the soil and water in the ground on which they grow. The animals eat the vegetation and plants and those atoms become part of their bodies. People eat the meat and other parts of the animals, and so those atoms are transferred to their bodies. Through procreation, those atoms are passed on to their children.

The human being is really a biological, mechanical, chemical, electrical, and electromagnetic being. As we know, life in the human being is the combination and interaction of biological, mechanical, chemical, electrical, and electromagnetic phenomena. The electromagnetic or the energy part is the most important aspect of life and the blueprint of life itself. After our physical death, the biological, chemical, electrical, and mechanical functions of our bodies cease to exist. What happens to the electromagnetic or energy part of the human being? The electromagnetic or energy part of our existence does not die, because that energy has a different form of existence. This is true according to the well-known scientific law of conservation of energy which states that energy may neither be created nor destroyed and, therefore, the sum of all the energies in the system is a constant. Thus, our essence or soul continues its existence even after our physical body is dead, and our journey continues. Rumi further explains that process in *Mathnavi* in more detail, which is presented in the next segment.

157

The Diverse Forms and Stages
of the Nature of Man from the Beginning

(Mathnavi Book 4, starting from Verse 3637)

آمده اوّل به اقلیم جماد

سالها اندر نباتی عمر کرد

و ز جمادی چون به حیوانی فتاد

جز همین میلی که دارد سوی آن

همچو میل کودکان با مادران

همچو میل مفرط هر نو مرید

جُزو عقل این از آن عقل کل است

سایه اش آخر شود فانی درو

سایه شاخ دگر ای نیکبخت

باز از حیوان سوی انسانیش

همچنین اقلیم تا اقلیم رفت

عقل های اوّلینش یاد نیست

تا رهد زین عقل پُر حرص و طلب

گر چه خفته گشت و شد ناسی ز پیش

باز از آن خوابش به بیداری کشند

که چه غم بود آنک می خوردم بخواب

چون ندانستم که آن غم و اعتلال

همچنان دنیا که حلم نایمست

تا بر آید ناگهان صبح اجل

خنده اش گیرد از آن غمهای خویش

هر چه تو در خواب بینی نیک و بد

آنچ کردی اندر این خواب جهان

تا نپنداری که این بد کردنیست

بلکه این خنده بود گریه و زَفیر

گریه و درد و غم و زاری خود

خون نخسبد بعد مرگت در قصاص

و ز جمادی در نباتی او فتاد

و ز جمادی یاد ناورد از نبرد

نامدش حال نباتی هیچ یاد

خاصه در وقت بهار و ضیمران

سِرِّ میل خود نداند در لبان

سوی آن پیر جوان بخت مجید

جنبش این سایه ز آن شاخ گل است

پس بداند سِرِّ میل و جست و جو

کی بجنبد گر نجنبد این درخت

می کشد آن خالقی که دانیش

تا شد اکنون عاقل و دانا و زفت

هم از این عقلش تحوّل کردنیست

صد هزاران عقل بیند بوالعجب

کی گذارندش در آن نسیان خویش

که کند بر حالت خود ریش خند

چون فراموشم شد احوال صواب

فعل خوابست و فریبست و خیال

خفته پندارد که این خود دایمست

وارهد از ظلمت ظنّ و دغل

چون ببیند مُستقَرّ و جای خویش

روز محشر یک بیک پیدا شود

گرددت هنگام بیداری عیان

اندرین خواب و ترا تعبیر نیست

روز تعبیر ای ستمگر بر اسیر

شادمانی دان ببیداری خود

تو مگو که مُردم و یابم خلاص

158

این قصاص نقد حیلت سازیست   پیش زخم آن قصاص این بازیست

زین لَعب خواندست دنیا را خدا   کین جزا لَعب است پیش آن جزا

این جزا تسکین جنگ و فتنه ایست

آن چو اِخصا است و این چون خَتنه ایست

He has come first to the world of the inanimate,
From the inanimate (state) fell into the vegetation (state).
For years he lived in the vegetation form,
And did not remember the inanimateness
because of the struggle (between states).
When he was transformed
from the vegetation to the animal (state),
He did not remember the state of vegetation at all.
Except the desire he has for that (vegetation),
Especially in the time of spring and sweet-smelling herbs.
Like the affection of babies for their mothers,
(The baby) does not know the secret of desire in his lips.
Similar to the excessive affection of a new disciple,
Toward that glorious fortunate Morad (guide).
His minor intellect is from that Universal Intellect (God),
The motion of this shadow is from that flower branch.
His shadow finally will disappear in him,
Then he will know the secret of his desire and search.
Oh, fortunate one, how can the shadow of another branch
Move if the tree will not move?
Again from the animal (state) toward the human (state),
That Creator that you know is taking him.
This way he went from world to world,
So now he has become wise and knowledgeable and strong.
He does not remember his former intelligences (memories),
From this (human) intelligence he will also evolve.
So he will escape from this intellect,
full of greed and desire,
He will surprisingly see a hundred thousand intelligences.
Even though he fell asleep and became forgetful of the past,
How would they leave him in his forgetfulness?
Again from that sleep they will drag him to wakefulness,
So he will laugh at his own state.

159

(Saying) "Why was I grieving in my sleep?
How did I forget my true status?
How did I not know that that sorrow and illness,
Is the function of sleep and is illusion and fantasy?
Similarly, this world which is the sleeper's dream,
The sleeper thinks that this is permanent.
Until suddenly the dawn of death arises,
And he is freed from the darkness of suspicion and deception.
He will laugh at his sorrows,
When he sees his eternal place and home.
Whatever you see good or bad in your dream (in this world),
One by one will appear in the Day of Justice.
Whatever you did in this sleep in the world,
Will appear to you at the time of awakening.
So you should not think,
that this evil act is permissible in this dream (world),
And has no consequence.
But this laughter will be cries and sighs,
On the day of interpretation,
oh, oppressor of the enslaved.
Your cries and pain and sorrow and lamentation,
You will know as jubilation in your awakening.
The blood (shed by you) will not sleep,
after your death in (the law of) retaliation,
Do not say that I will die and I will be freed.
This present retaliation (in the present world)
is a (temporary) deception,
In comparison with the wound of that (future) retaliation,
this is a play.
For this, God has called this world a play,
Because this punishment is a play,
in comparison with that punishment.
This punishment is a (temporary) relief for war and strife,
That (punishment) is like castration,
and this one is like circumcision.

Rumi further explains in the above verses that our present life in this present world is like a dream. After passing from this world, in the next world we will feel that we just woke up from a long, deep sleep. We will see the results and effects of our actions and deeds during our physical life on the planet Earth, which was like a dream state. Therefore, we will be faced with the real consequences of our conduct, from which we may have escaped or for which we may have received only partial punishment on the Earth. We will also laugh at the worries, sorrows, and fears we had in our earthly life once we learn about our new world and realize that our life is continual and eternal. Rumi reminds us that we should not think that our wrong actions have no consequences; instead, in the continuation of our journey, we have to face and deal with whatever we have done in our present physical life.

The Nature of Human Beings

(Mathnavi, Book 4, starting from Verse 1189)

زآنک قُوت و نان ستون جان بود   آدمی اوّل حریص نان بود

جان نهاده بر کف از حرص و اَمل   سوی کسب و سوی غصب و صد حیل

عاشق نامست و مدح شاعران   چون به نادر گشت مُستغنی ز نان

در بیان فضل او منبر نهند   تا که اصل و قصل او را بر دهند

همچو عنبر بو دهد در گفت و گو   تا که فَرّ و کَرّ و زر بخشیٔ او

وصف ما گیرد ز وصف او سَبَق   خَلق ما بر صورت خود کرد حق

آدمی را مدح جویی نیز خوست   چونک آن خلاق شکرو حمد جوست

The human being is first greedy for bread,
Because food and bread are the pillars of life.
In pursuit of business and usurpation (seizure of property),
with a hundred tricks,
He has put his life on his palm from greed and desire.
When rarely he becomes needless of bread (material things),
He is in love with fame and praise of the poets.
So they adorn his root and branch (nature and virtue),
And from the pulpit express his superiority.
So his glory and majesty and gold-giving generosity,
Will smell like ambergris (perfume) in the conversation.
God created us in God's own image,
Our characteristics are modeled upon God's characteristics.
Since the Creator desires thanksgiving and glorification,
Consequently desiring praise is also the nature of man.

(Mathnavi Book 3, starting from Verse1000)

از فزونی آمد و شد   در کمی   خویشتن نشناخت مسکین آدمی

بود اطلس خویش بر دلقی بدوخت   خویشتن را آدمی ارزان فروخت

Pitiful Man did not appreciate himself,
He came from more and became less.

Man sold himself cheap,
He was (like) satin, but sewed himself on to a rag.

(Mathnavi Book 1, starting from verse1581)

لا مکانی فوق فهم سالکان   صورتش بر خاک و جان بر لا مکان

هر دمی در وی خیالی زایدت   لا مکانی نی که در فهم آیدت

همچو در حکم بهشتی چار جو   بل مکان و لا مکان در حکم او

His face (body) from the soil and his soul from eternity,
An eternity beyond the comprehension
of the travelers (mystics).
An eternity which would not fit in your thoughts,
And every moment a thought would be born in it.
Every place and eternity under God's command,
Like the paradise with four streams.

(Mathnavi Book 3, starting from Verse 2648)

می نداند جان خود را آن ظلوم   صد هزاران فضل داند از علوم

در بیان جوهر خود چون خری   داند او خاصیت هر جوهری

خود ندانی تو یَجُوزی یا عَجُوز   که همی دانم یَجُوز و لا یَجُوز

تو روا یا نا روایی بین تو نیک   این روا آن ناروا دانی و لیک

قیمت خود را ندانی احمقیست   قیمت هر کاله می دانی که چیست

ننگری تو سعدی یا ناشُسته‌ٔ   سعدها و نحس‌ها دانسته‌ٔ

که بدانی من کیم در یوم دین   جان جمله علمها اینست این

بنگر اندر اصل خود گر هست نیک   آن أصول دین بدانستی تو لیک

که بدانی اصل خود ای مَرد مِه   از أصولینت أصول خویش به

He knows a hundred thousand subjects
from different sciences,
But he does not know his own soul out of ignorance.
He knows about the essence of almost everything,
But in understanding his own essence,
he is like a donkey.

163

(He says) I know permissible and impermissible,
But you do not know if you are permissible or an old witch.
You know this just and that unjust,
But, look carefully if you are just or unjust.
You know the value of every material good,
Not knowing the value of yourself is foolishness.
You have known fortunate and unfortunate,
But you do not look at yourself
to see if you are fortunate or unpolished.
The essence of all science is this,
That you will know who you are on the Day of Judgment.
You know the fundamentals of the religion,
Look at your own essence to see if it is good.
From the fundamentals your own fundamental is better,
So you will know who you are, oh great man.

The Caravan of Life

(Mathnavi Book 1, starting from Verse1886)

از خزینه قدرت تو کی گریخت   قطره ای کو در هوا شد یا بریخت

چون بخوانیش او کند از سَرِ قدم   گر درآید در عدم یا صد عدم

بازشان حکم تو بیرون می کِشد   صد هزاران ضِدّ ضِد را می کُشد

هست یارب کاروان در کاروان   از عدمها سوی هستی هر زمان

A drop that vaporized in the air
or poured down (on the Earth),
How can it escape from the treasure of Your power?
If it becomes nothing or a hundred nothings,
If You (God) summon it, it will rise with its head.
A hundred thousand of opposites kill their opposites,
Again Your command will bring them out (alive).
Every moment, flowing from nothingness toward existence,
Oh God, there is caravan after caravan.

As I stated earlier, this world is made of opposing forces and natures that are continuously confronting each other. However, the Almighty's power is the only force in the universe that allows anything to be destroyed or come into existence again. We only look at this world from the very narrow bandwidth of the red to violet frequency spectrum. We only see things that are in our confined range of vision of visible light. What we do not see, does not mean it does not exist. It could simply be that we are not capable of seeing it. Due to our limitations, we in fact only observe the caravan of life or existence from our narrow window of vision. We do not know at any moment who comes into this world and who leaves. We do not know at any second who dies and who is born.

CHAPTER 3

DIVINE

DESTINY

Divine Destiny and Regrets

Rumi skillfully describes how Divine Destiny hides from us the flaws of our thoughts and actions so we can carry on in accordance with Divine Destiny. He also expresses why we should not regret the past or waste our time and energy and especially our mental health and happiness because of mistakes we have made in the past. In different books of *Mathnavi*, Rumi expounds on this subject. The verses below are some examples:

(Mathnavi Book 4, starting from Verse 1332)

تو بِجِد کاری که بگرفتی بدست   عیشِ این دم بر تو پوشیده شدست

زان همی تانی بدادن تن بکار   که بپوشید از تو عیبش کردگار

همچنین هر فکر که گرمی در آن   عیب آن فکرت شدست از تو نهان

بر تو گر پیدا شدی زو عیب و شَین   زو رمیدی جانت بُعدَ المَشرقَین

حال کآخر زو پشیمان می شوی   گر بود این حالت اوّل کی دوی

پس بپوشید اوّل آن بر جان ما   تا کنیم آن کار بر وفق قضا

چون قضا آورد حکم خود پدید   چشم وا شد تا پشیمانی رسید

این پشیمانی قضای دیگر است   این پشیمانی بِهل حق را پرست

ور کنی عادت پشیمان خور شوی   زین پشیمانی پشیمان تر شوی

نیم عمرت در پریشانی رود   نیم دیگر در پشیمانی رود

ترک این فکر و پشیمانی بگو   فعل و کار و یار نیکوتر بجو

ور نداری کار نیکوتر بدست   پس پشیمانیت از بهر چه است

Whenever you have seriously taken a work in hand,
Its inadequacy is veiled to you at that moment.
Since the Creator covered its faultiness from you,
From that you are able to give yourself up to the work.
Similarly, every thought that you are hot about,
The flaw of that thought is hidden from you.
If its error and shame were apparent to you,
Your soul would flee from it as far as possible.
Now that you are regretful about that ending,
Would you have tried,

if you had this state of mind in the beginning?
Therefore, God veils that from our soul at first,
So we perform that task in accordance with (Divine) destiny.
When (Divine) destiny revealed its decree,
The eye was opened and regret arrived.
This regret is another fate,
Renounce this regret and praise God.
If you make a habit and become addicted to regret,
From this regret you become more regretful.
Half of your life will pass in despair,
The other half will pass in regret.
Desert this thought and regret,
Seek a better situation, friend, and work.
If you have no better work in hand,
Then what is your regret for?

(Mathnavi Book 4, continuing from Verse 1349)

تو ز عیب آن حجابی اندری	همچنین هر آرزو که می بری
خود رمیدی جان تو از جستجو	ور نمودی علّت آن آرزو
کس نبردی کش کشان آن سو ترا	گر نمودی عیب آن کار او ترا
زآن بود که عیش آمد در ظهور	وآن دگر کاری کز آن هستی نفور
عیب کار بد ز ما پنهان مکن	ای خدای راز دان خوش سخن
تا نگردیم از روش سرد و هبا	عیب کار نیک را مَنما بما

Likewise, whatever dream you pursue,
You are unaware of its imperfection.
And if the flaw of that desire was shown,
Your soul would have abandoned that search.
If God had shown you the flaw of that work,
No one could have taken you in that direction.
Oh God, aware of secrets and marvelous in speech,
Don't hide from us the flaw of bad deeds.
Do not show us the flaw of good deeds,
So we will not become cold and distracted
in the path (of doing that deed).

In other profound verses Rumi further discusses regrets:

(Mathnavi Book 1, starting from Verse 1711)

از وجود نقد خود بُریدن است   این دریغاها خیال دیدن است

کو دلی کز عشق حق صد پاره نیست   غیرت حق بود و با حق چاره نیست

> *This regretfulness is the illusion of vision,*
> *It is departing from your present existence.*
> *It is God's will and there is no escape from it,*
> *Where is a heart that is not torn*
> *into a hundred pieces from God's love?*

(Mathnavi Book 1, starting from Verse 2201)

ماضی و مُستَقبَلت پردهٔ خدا   هست هشیاری ز یاد مامَضیٰ

پرگره باشی‌ازین دو همچو نی   آتش اندر زن بهر دو تا به کی

همنشین آن لب و آواز نیست   تا گره با نی بود همراز نیست

> *Awareness is from recollection of what is past,*
> *The past and the future conceal God from you.*
> *Set fire to both,*
> *until when,*
> *Are you full of obstacles like a blocked reed?*
> *If a reed is blocked,*
> *It is not the companion of the lips and song.*

(Mathnavi Book 3, starting from Verse 3616)

اوّل آتش در پشیمانی زند   گر پشیمانی بر او عیبی کند

گر ببیند گرمی صاحب قدم   خود پشیمانی نروید از عدم

> *If regret would scold him,*
> *First, he would set fire to the regret.*
> *The regret itself would not come into existence*

from nothingness,
If it sees the passion of the traveler (on the path of love).

A significant part of our lives is wasted on regretting what we should have, could have, and would have done. We go through a lot of anger and mental and emotional pain because of that regretfulness. We usually torture ourselves and bother our mates, friends, and others by thinking and talking about what we have done wrong, wishing that we had done things differently. If we stop for a moment and try to look at each situation as an impartial observer and be objective about what has happened, we should realize that the past has gone and we can do nothing about it. The future has not come, so why should we worry about it? God willing, with positive thinking, energy, and imagery, most probably everything will turn out in our favor anyway. By dwelling on the past which we can do nothing about, and worrying about a future which has not even come, we are only wasting our time and good and positive energy. In the process we are also damaging our mental and physical health. Think about any event about which you were really concerned. Regardless of how much you suffered and tortured yourself, the outcome was the same as if you had never worried and wasted your precious time and happiness.

Destined to Make Mistakes

(Mathnavi Book 1, starting from Verse 1248)

گر ستایم تا قیامت قاصرم   این چنین آدم که نامش می بَرم

دانش یک نهی شد بر وی خطا   این همه دانست و چون آمد قضا

یا بتأویلی بُد و تُوهیم بود   کای عجب نهی از پی تحریم بود

طبع در حیرت سوی گندم شتافت   در دلش تأویل چون ترجیح یافت

Adam, who I am mentioning,
If I praise him until the Resurrection Day, I fall short.
He knew it all, but when (Divine)Destiny came,
Even in the knowledge of a single prohibition he was at fault.
Amazingly, was the prohibition for the purpose of forbidding,
Or was it an interpretation and suspicion?
Since the interpretation in his heart prevailed,
In confusion, his nature rushed toward the wheat (apple).

(Mathnavi Book 2, starting from Verse 15)

شد فراق صدر جنت طوق نفس   یک قدم زد آدم اندر ذوق نفس

بهر نانی چند آب چشم ریخت   همچو دیو از وی فرشته می گریخت

لیک آن مو در دو دیده رسته بود   گر چه یک مو بُد گُنه کو جسته بود

موی در دیده بود کوه عظیم   بود آدم دیدهٔ نور قدیم

در پشیمانی نگفتی معذرت   گر در آن آدم بکردی مشورت

Adam took one step in following his sensual desire,
The separation from (his) high place in paradise,
became the chain for his soul.
The angels were fleeing from him,
like fleeing from a devil;
How many tears did he shed for some bread?
Even though the sin he had committed was (as thin as) a hair,
But the hair had grown in the eyes.

Adam was the eye of the Eternal Light (God),
A hair in the eye is like a great mountain.
If Adam had consulted (God) about that,
He would not have uttered apologies in regret.

(Mathnavi Book3, starting from Verse 469)

عاقلان گردند جمله کور و کر	چون قضا بیرون کند از چرخ سَر
دام گیرد مرغ پَرّان را زبون	ماهیان افتند از دریا برون
بلکه هاروتی ببابل در رود	تا پری و دیو در شیشه شود
خون او را هیچ تربیعی نریخت	جز کسی کاندر قضا اندر گریخت
هیچ حیله ندهدت از وی رها	غیر آنک در گریزی در قضا

When Divine Destiny puts forth its head from heaven,
All the wise become blind and deaf.
The fishes are thrown out of the sea,
The trap catches the ill-fated flying bird.
Even the genie and devil go into the bottle,
Even Harut goes into the pit of Babylon.
Except someone who sought refuge in Divine Destiny,
No astrological alignment could shed his blood.
Unless you seek refuge in Divine Destiny,
no treachery will free you from it.

Rumi cleverly uses the story of Adam as a metaphor to describe Divine Destiny. Almighty God had taught Adam knowledge and granted him such a high position that even the angels and Lucifer had to bow to him. Nevertheless, when Divine Destiny arrived, even Adam, with all of his wisdom and insight, could not escape.

In the same manner, we all are also prone to err in accordance with Divine Destiny. Later in life we might learn that the mistakes we made were for the higher purpose of learning and our enlightenment in our journey of life. Every individual has a special path tailored for him or her. Each of us travels through our own path no matter if we crawl, or walk, or run, or fly. Your path will have a wonderful ending, if you realize that life is a magnificent, continual journey. Do not let the time in this present life pass by without taking maximum advantage of it. Do not waste your time and life on regrets and reservations about the past. Try to be joyful and happy that you are alive and have the level of understanding that you have attained. Be hopeful that God's mercy and benevolence will forever be upon you.

174

Being at Peace with the World

(Mathnavi Book 1, Verse 1570)

بُوالعَجَب من عاشق این هردو ضد   عاشقم بر قهر و بر لطفش بجد

I am truly in love with God's grace and wrath ,
What a wonder, I am in love with these two opposites.

(Mathnavi Book 4, starting from Verse 3262)

این جهان چون جنتستم در نظر   من که صُلحم دائماً با این پدر
تا ز نو دیدن فرو میرد ملال   هر زمان نو صورتی و نو جمال
آبها از چشمه ها جوشان مُقیم   من همی بینم جهانرا پُر نعیم
مست می گردد ضمیر و هوش من   بانگ آبش می رسد در گوش من
برگها کف زن مثال مُطربان   شاخها رقصان شده چون تایبان

I am always at peace with the Father (of the universe),
This world is like paradise in my eyes.
Every time new features, new beauties,
So from seeing new (things), sorrow would perish.
I see the world full of bounties,
Waters continuously flowing from the springs.
The sound of water comes to my ears,
My conscious (soul) and intellect become intoxicated.
The branches are dancing like penitents,
Leaves clapping like the minstrels.

(Mathnavi Book 4, starting from Verse 3259)

کوست بابای هر آنک اهل قُل است   کُل عالم صورت عقل کُل است
صورت کُل پیش او هم سگ نمود   چون کسی با عقل کُل کفران فزود

175

صُلح کن با این پدر عاقی بِهل   تا که فرش زر نماید آب و گِل

پس قیامت نقد حالِ تو بُوَد   پیش تو چرخ و زمین مُبدَل شود

The entire universe is the face of Universal Wisdom (God),
The Father of whomever is a follower of the Divine Word.
When someone denied Universal Wisdom (God),
The shape of the universe appeared to him as a dog.
Make peace with the Father,
give up disobedience,
So the water and soil appear (to you) as a gold carpet.
Then the Resurrection Day will become
the state of your present being,
The universe and the Earth will be altered in front of you.

Beyond Soil, Water, Wind, Fire, Heaven, and Earth

In the succeeding poem Rumi eloquently describes his absolute devotion to his beloved, the Supreme Creator:

(Kollyyate Divane Shams, Monshi Nool Edition, India, 1923)

چه تدبیر ای مسلمانان که من خود را نمیدانم
نه ترسا نه یهودم من نه گبر و نه مسلمانم

نه شرقیّم نه غربیّم نه بریّم نه بحریّم
نه از کان طبیعتم نه از افلاک گردانم

نه از هندم نه از چینم نه از بلغار و سقسینم
نه از مُلک عراقینم نه از خاک خراسانم

نه از خاکم نه از آبم نه از بادم نه از آتش
نه از عرشم نه از فرشم نه از کونم نه از کانم

نه از دنیا نه از عقبیٰ نه از جنت نه از دوزخ
نه از آدم نه از حوا نه از فردوس و رضوانم

هوالاول هو الاخر هوالظاهر هوالباطن
که من جز هو و یا من هو کس دیگر نمی دانم

مکانم لا مکان باشد نشانم بی نشان باشد
نه تن باشد نه جان باشد که من از جان جانانم

دوئی را چون برون کردم دو عالم را یکی دیدم
یکی بینم یکی جویم یکی دانم یکی خوانم

اگر در عمر خود روزی دمی بی تو بر آوردم
از آنروز و از آن ساعت پشیمانم پشیمانم

ز جام عشق سر مستم دو عالم رفته از دستم
بجز رندی و قلاشی نباشد هیچ سامانم

اگر دستم دهد روزی دمی با تو در این خلوت
دو عالم زیر پای آرم همی دستی برافشانم

الا ای شمس تبریزی چنان مستم در این عالم
که جز مستی و سر مستی دگر چیزی نمی دانم

Oh, dear Moslems,
what a pity that I do not know myself,
I am not a Jew nor a Christian,
not a Zoroastrian nor a Moslem.
I am not from the East nor from the West,
not from the land nor from the sea;
I am not from Mother Nature
nor from the spinning galaxies.
I am not from India nor from China,
not from Bulgaria nor from Saghseen,
I am not from Iraq nor from Khorasan.
I am not from the soil nor from the water,
not from the wind nor from the fire;
I am not from the sky nor from the (earth's) carpet,
not from existence nor from nature.
I am not from this world nor from the hereafter,
not from heaven nor from hell;
I am not from Adam nor from Eve,
not from the Garden of Eden nor from paradise.
God is first, God is last,
God is outward, God is inward;
Except for God or from God,
I know no one.
My home is beyond any place,
my place is beyond any address,

178

It's not the body,
it's not the soul,
I am from the dearest of the dears,
the soul of the Supreme Creator.
I rid myself from duality and see both worlds as one,
I see one ,
I seek one,
I know one,
I call one.
If in my life one day,
I took even a breath without You (God),
From that day and that hour of my life,
I am regretful, I am regretful.
I am intoxicated with the wine of love,
both worlds have fallen out of my hands,
Except libertinism and tippling (drunkenness),
I have no welfare.
If one day a moment with you in seclusion,
comes to my hand,
I put both worlds under my feet,
I dance with all of my being.
Oh, Shams of Tabriz,
I am so drunken in this world,
That except drunkenness and joyfulness,
I know nothing else.

Divine Destiny Cannot Be Escaped

There is a fascinating and profound fable in the first book of *Mathnavi*. To escape from Divine Destiny, a man went to holy Solomon and asked for his help. This man thought he could flee from a destined death that he had assumed would occur in a certain place in accordance with his imagination and thoughts. In reality, he was asking holy Solomon to make something possible which ordinarily would have been impossible for him. In other words, thinking he could escape from Divine Destiny, he actually ended up begging holy Solomon to make it possible for him to travel all the way to India just to follow that Divine Destiny. From this story it should be apparent that what we think might be beneficial and good for us, in reality might be a wish for our own destruction.

(Mathnavi Book 1, starting from Verse 959)

زاد مردی چاشتگاهی در رسید   در سرا عدلِ سلیمان در دوید

رویش از غم زرد و هر دو لب کبود   پس سلیمان گفت ای خواجه چه بود

گفت عزرائیل در من این چنین   یک نظر انداخت پُر از خشم و کین

گفت هین اکنون چه میخواهی بخواه   گفت فرما باد را ای جان پناه

تا مرا زینجا بهندُستان بَرَد   بُوک بنده کآن طرف شد جان بَرَد

باد را فرمود تا او را شتاب   بُرد سوی قعر هندُستان بر آب

روز دیگر وقت دیدار و لقا   پس سلیمان گفت عزرائیل را

کآن مسلمان را بخشم از بهر آن   بنگریدی تا شد آواره ز خوان

گفت از خشم من کی کردم نظر   از تعجب دیدمش در ره گذر

که مرا فرمود حق امروز هان   جان او را تو بهندُستان سِتان

از عجب گفتم گر او را صد پَرَست   او بهندُستان شدن دور اندرست

تو همه کار جهان را همچنین   کن قیاس و چشم بُگشا و ببین

A righteous man one morning,
Ran to (holy) Solomon's court of justice.
From sorrow his face was yellow and his lips black and blue,
Then (holy) Solomon said, "Oh, Khajeh (Mr.) what is it?"

He said, "Azrael (angel of death) took a look at me,
With anger and vengeance."
He (Solomon) said, "Now what do you want? Ask,"
He said, "Order the wind, oh, guardian of life.
To take me to India from here,
So this servant would save his life by going there."
(Solomon) Ordered the wind to take him quickly,
Deep inside India over the water.
The next day in the court at the time of visiting,
Solomon said to Azrael:
"Why did you look at that believer with anger,
To make him a refugee (far) from his home?"
Azrael said, "When did I look at him with anger?
I looked at him with amazement on the road.
The Almighty commanded me that today,
I should take his life in India.
I said from amazement that,
if he even had a hundred feathers (wings),
His going to India is far from reality."
You should look at the world affairs in the same way,
Open your eyes and see.

Be Careful What You Wish For

In another insightful story in the second book of *Mathnavi*, Rumi tells of a thief who steals a snake from a snake charmer. The snake bites the thief, who dies painfully. The snake charmer happens to pass by and see the dead thief. He says to himself, "I was praying that I would find him and take my snake back. I am so grateful to God that my prayer was not accepted and as a result I am still alive. I thought that prayer was to my benefit, but in fact it would have destroyed me." Below are the verses in which Rumi tells the story:

(Mathnavi Book 2, starting from Verse 135)

دزدکی از مارگیری مار برد   ز ابلهی آنرا غنیمت می شمرد

وارهید آن مارگیر از زخم مار   مارکُشت آن دزد او را زار زار

مارگیرش دید پس بشناختش   گفت از جان مار من پرداختش

در دعا می خواستی جانم از او   کش بیابم مار بستانم ازو

شکر حق را کآن دعا مردود شد   من زیان پنداشتم آن سود شد

بس دعاها کآن زیان است و هلاک   از کَرَم می نشنود یزدان پاک

A petty thief stole a snake from a snake charmer,
From foolishness he assumed that it was a treasure.
The snake charmer was saved from the snake's wound,
The snake killed that thief painfully.
The snake charmer saw and recognized him (the thief),
He said, "My snake took his life.
In my prayer I was asking to find him,
And take my snake back.
Thank the Almighty that my prayer was rejected,
And what I thought was a loss became a benefit."
Many prayers that are damaging and destructive,
From mercy, the pure God does not listen to them.

Our Sustenance or Daily Provisions

Rumi teaches the concept of sustenance (Rezgh) throughout the *Mathnavi*, especially in the following verses:

(Mathnavi Book 5, starting from Verse 2385)

در فرو بسته ست و بر در قفلها   گفت پیغمبر که بر رزق ای فتا

هست مفتاحی بر آن و قفل و حجاب   جنبش و آمد شد ما و اکتساب

بی طلب نان سنت الله نیست   بی کلید این در گشادن راه نیست

The holy Prophet said to sustenance, "Oh young one,
The door is closed and there are locks on the door.
Our effort and movement and seeking,
Are the keys to that lock and cover.
Without the key, there is no way to open the door,
Without effort, giving bread is not the tradition of Allah."

(Mathnavi Book 5, Verse 2391)

جمله را رَزّاق روزی می دهد   قسمت هر یک بپیشش می نهد

The Provider (God) grants daily provisions to everyone,
(God) places each one's share before him.

(Mathnavi Book 5, Verse 2395)

هر کسی را کی رسد گنج نهفت   چون قناعت را پیمبر گنج گفت

تا نیفتی در نشیب شور و شَر   حد خود بشناس و بر بالا مپر

Since the Prophet called contentment a treasure,
How can everyone reach the hidden treasure?
Know your limit and do not jump high,
So you will not slide on the slope of trouble and hassle.

(Mathnavi Book 5, Verse 2400)

آنچنانک عاشقی بر رزق زار   هست عاشق رزق هم بر رزق خوار

*The same way that you are passionately in love
with your sustenance,
Similarly, the sustenance is in love with you (the consumer).*

(Mathnavi Book 6, Verse 1930)

گر بیابان پُر شود زرّ و نقود   بی رضای حق جوئی نتوان ربود

*If the desert becomes full of gold and cash,
Without God's permission even a grain cannot be taken.*

(Mathnavi Book 5, Verse 2851)

هین توکل کن ملرزان پا و دست   رزق تو بر تو ز تو عاشق تر است

*Go depend on God and don't let your hands and feet tremble,
Your sustenance is more in love with you
than you are with yourself.*

Rumi explains the meaning of dependence on God
through a perceptive story about a righteous man who wanted to
test the concept of destined sustenance. This man traveled far
away from the city without any provisions to an isolated
mountain. Since he was hungry, he rested his head on a stone.
He was saying to himself, "I depend on you, God, to provide my
sustenance and the means of it. I cut off other means so I can see
the result of my dependency on the Almighty." The following is
an excerpt from that story:

184

آن یکی زاهد شنود از مصطفیٰ — که یقین آید بجان رزق از خدا

گر بخواهی ور نخواهی رزق تو — پیش تو آید دوان از عشق تو

از برای امتحان آن مرد رفت — در بیابان نزد کوهی خُفت تَفت

که ببینم رزق می آید بمن — تا قوی گردد مرا در رزق ظن

کاروانی راه گم کرد و کشید — سوی کوه آن ممتحن را خفته دید

گفت این مرد این طرف چونست عور — در بیابان از ره و از شهر دور

ای عجب مرده ست یا زنده که او — می نترسد هیچ از گرگ و عدو

آمدند و دست بر وی می زدند — قاصداً چیزی نگفت آن ارجمند

هم نجبید و نجنبانید سر — وانکرد از امتحان هم او بصر

پس بگفتند این ضعیف بی مُراد — از مجاعت سکته اندر اوفتاد

نان بیاوردند و در دیگی طعام — تا بریزندش بحلقوم و بکام

پس بقاصد مرد دندان سخت کرد — تا ببیند صدق آن میعاد مرد

رحمشان آمد که این بس بی نواست — وزمجاعت هالک مرگ و فناست

کارد آوردند قوم اشتاقتند — بسته دندانهاش را بشکافتند

ریختند اندر دهانش شوربا — می فشردند اندرو نان پاره ها

گفت ای دل گر چه خود تن می زنی — راز می دانی و نازی می کنی

گفت دل دانم و قاصد می کنم — رزاق الله است بر جان و تنم

امتحان زین بیشتر خود چون بود — رزق سوی صابران خوش می رود

A righteous man heard from the Chosen One (the Prophet),
That definitely sustenance comes to your life,
from the Almighty.
Your sustenance, whether you desire or not,
Comes to you running with love.
For an experiment that man went to the desert,
Near a mountain and slept fast.
(Saying)So I'll see if my sustenance comes to me,
Then my belief will become stronger about (my) sustenance.
A caravan lost its way and came
Toward the mountain and saw that man sleeping.
Somebody said, "How is this man destitute
In the wilderness, far from road and city?
Oh, I wonder if he is dead or alive,

Isn't he afraid of wolves or enemies?"
They came and were touching him with their hands,
That man did not say anything on purpose.
He did not move or turn his head,
He did not open his eyes for the experiment.
Then they said, "This weak and hopeless man,
From hunger must have passed out."
They brought bread and food in a pot,
To pour into his mouth and stomach.
The man intentionally clenched his teeth,
So he could see the truth about that promise (of sustenance).
They felt sorry for him that he must be very weak,
And from hunger he was perishing and dying.
They hurried and brought a knife,
And opened his clenched teeth.
They poured soup into his mouth,
They squeezed pieces of bread into him.
The man said, "Oh my heart,
even though you are being silent,
You know the truth but are playing ignorant."
His heart said, "I know, but I am doing this intentionally,
God is the provider (of sustenance) for my soul and body.
Can there be any test more than this?
The sustenance goes toward the patient one beautifully."

The Sufis believe that when you are born, the Master Creator (praise be to God) has given you a time, a predetermined period to live on this Earth as part of your life journey. Additionally, they believe that you are given your sustenance, which is your individual package or your *Rezgh*. This Rezgh is not only the material wealth that is supposed to come to you, but actually the collection of all you are given in this world. Your genes, looks, health, talents, wealth, and everything else are included in your Rezgh.

If you ever really look at the past, you will see a lot of wonderful opportunities and amazing events that occurred without any prior plan or intention. Sometimes it just happened that you were there at the right time and in the right place and

186

everything worked for your best interest. Therefore, instead of worrying and exhausting your mind about how to do this or that, it is better that you put your trust in your Supreme Maker and accept your Divine Destiny and not worry. It is actually more beneficial for you to calm down and allow yourself to use your spiritual power by depending on the Divine Power who controls everything. Do your best, but do not be anxious about the outcome since your Rezgh is also seeking you. This way of thinking will bring an amazing feeling of serenity and peace to your life. You will feel that you are not alone and have now tapped into the incredible, infinite power of the universe and its Divine Creator which is beyond anyone's imagination and control.

The Story of Holy Jesus and the Fool

In the next poem, Rumi relates a fascinating story about a foolish man who asked holy Jesus (peace and blessings be upon him) to teach him the prayer that holy Jesus used to revive the dead and cure crippled and ill people.

(Mathnavi Book 2, starting from Verse141)

گشت با عیسی یکی ابله رفیق   استخوانها دید در حُفره عمیق

گفت ای همره تو آن نام سَنی   که بدان تو مرده زنده می‌کنی

مر مرا آموز تا احسان کنم   استخوانها را بدآن با جان کنم

گفت خامُش کن که آن کار تو نیست   لایق انفاس و گفتار تو نیست

کآن نَفَس خواهد ز باران پاک تر   وز فرشته در رَوش دَرّاک تر

عمرها بایست تا دم پاک شد   تا امین مخزن افلاک شد

گفت اگر من نیستم اسرار خوان   هم تو بر خوان نام را بر استخوان

گفت عیسی یارب این اسرار چیست   میل این ابله در این بیگار چیست

چون غم خود نیست این بیمار را   چون غم جان نیست این مردار را

مُرده خود را رها کردست او   مُرده بیگانه را جوید رفو

گفت حقّ اِدبار اگر اِدبار جُوست   تخم روئیده جزای کِشتِ اوست

آنک تخم خار کارد در جهان   هان و هان او را مجو در گُلستان

A foolish man became (holy) Jesus' companion,
He saw some bones in a deep hole.
He said, "Oh my companion (holy Jesus),
that exalted name (prayer),
Which you revive the dead with.
Teach me so I can be generous,
And give life to those bones."
Holy Jesus said, "Be quiet, this is not your job,
Your words and your breath are not worthy of that.
That needs a breath purer than the rain,
And in action, swifter than angels.
It would take (many) lifetimes,
for the breath to become purified,

And become entrusted with the treasure of the universe."
He said, "If I am not worthy of reciting that secret prayer,
Then you recite that name (prayer) at those bones."
Holy Jesus said, "Oh, my God, what is the secret to this?
What is the desire of this foolish (man) in this useless work?
How is this ill person not concerned with himself?
How is this dead person not worried about his own soul?
He has left his own dead self,
He seeks to revive a dead stranger.
Whoever plants the seeds of shrubs in the world,
Do not look for him in a rose garden."

The tale has an unexpected ending. Finally, due to the foolish man's persistence, holy Jesus revives the dead bones with his prayer. The bones are turned into an aggressive lion that kills the man immediately.

(Mathnavi Book 2, continuing from Verse 456)

از برای التماس آن جوان	خواند عیسی نام حقّ بر استخوان
صورت آن استخوان را زنده کرد	حکم ایزد از پی آن خام مرد
پنجه‌ٔ زد کرد نقشش را تباه	از میان بر جست یک شیر سیاه
مغز جوزی کاندرو مغزی نبود	کلّه‌اش بر کند مغزش ریخت زود

Holy Jesus prayed over those bones in the name of God,
For the sake of that young man's begging.
God's destiny for that foolish man,
Revived those bones.
A dark lion jumped from those dead bones,
He pounced on him and ruined his existence.
Cut his head and smashed his brain...

(Mathnavi Book 2, continuing from Verse 462)

گفت زآن رو که تو زو آشوفتی	گفت عیسی چون شتابش کوفتی
گفت در قسمت نبودم رزق خورد	گفت عیسی چون نخوردی خون مرد
بود خالص از برای اعتبار	گفت آن شیر ای مسیحا در شکار
خود چه کارستی مرا با مردگان	گر مرا روزی بُدی اندر جهان

189

(Holy) Jesus said, "How did you maul him so quickly?"
The lion said, "Because you were bothered by him."
(Holy) Jesus said, "Why didn't you drink his blood?"
The lion said, "In my destiny,
it was not part of my sustenance."
The lion said, "Oh, Messiah,
this prey was purely for a lesson (to others).
If there was more sustenance for me in the world,
How should I have died?"

Several deep meanings are hidden in this dramatic and profound parable. The first concerns a man who is not aware of his own dead being, but wants to revive someone else. How true this is! We have forgotten about our own dying essence that we have not nurtured due to our ignorance, and yet we have the audacity to desire to do something for someone else that we have not been capable of doing for ourselves. The second meaning is about the predestined provision and sustenance of this world, which has been allotted to us. The story explains that no one has a bigger share outside of what has been divinely prearranged. Since the lion had completely received his share before dying, and the man was not a part of his preordained sustenance, the lion could not eat him. Also, the lion did not drink the man's blood because it was not a part of his sustenance. Finally, the man had to beg Jesus to bring the lion back to life so the lion would take his life. This illustrates our inability to escape from our Divine Destiny. If it were destined, we would seek with persistence our own destruction and make it possible through our insistence.

CHAPTER 4

RELATING TO GOD

If You Desire Paradise,
Do Not Ask Anything from Anyone

(Mathnavi Book 6, starting from Verse 333)

گفت پیغمبر که جنت از اِله   گرهمی‌خواهی زکس‌چیزی مخواه

چون نخواهی من کفیلم مر ترا   جنت المأوی و دیدار خدا

ور بأَمر حق بخواهی آن رواست   آن چنان خواهش طریق انبیاست

The holy Prophet said, "If you wish paradise from God,
Do not wish anything from anyone else.
If you do so, I will be your advocate,
That paradise will be your place and you will meet God.
But if you ask because of God's command, that is proper,
That kind of request is the way of the prophets."

(Mathnavi Book 5, starting from Verse 700)

من نخواهم دایه مادر خوشتر است   موسی‌ام من دایه من مادر است

من نخواهم لطف مَه از واسطه   که هلاک قوم شد این رابطه

I do not desire the nanny,
Mother is better;
I am like (holy) Moses,
my nanny is Mother.
I do not desire (God's) mercy from the intermediary,
Since this (intermediary) relation
became the destruction of the people.

The Story of Holy Moses and the Shepherd

Another profound story in the second book of *Mathnavi* is about holy Moses. In this tale, holy Moses came across a shepherd in the mountains who was talking to God. The shepherd was telling God that he wished he could comb God's hair, wash God's feet, and warm some milk for God so God could drink it. He was talking as if God were a human being, in need of physical care. Moses told the shepherd that the way he was praising God made God seem like a needy, little human being. He stated that this was blasphemy and the shepherd should stop doing it. Holy Moses cautioned that the Earth and the sky could burn from his blasphemy. The shepherd brokenheartedly realized that Moses was right, apologized, and ran away.

After a little while, Moses received a revelation from the Almighty, reproaching him for his actions. He was told that he was given the message and mission to connect people and bring them closer to God, not to create distance between people and God. Furthermore, it was explained to Moses that God looks inside peoples' hearts and sees their intention, purity, and sincerity. God does not care about the outward pretence and the play of their tongues. Thus, holy Moses was ordered to run after the shepherd.

Moses found the shepherd and told him that he had a wonderful message for him. Moses informed him not to worry, and pray in any way that he pleased. Holy Moses relayed to the shepherd that it would be fine to say anything he wished straight from his heart, directly to the Almighty. The shepherd responded that Moses need not worry. He explained that the pain and sorrow which was inflicted on him became a vehicle that transported him to a magnificent state and allowed him to soar so high, that nothing mattered anymore. The following are verses from the text of that story:

دید موسی یک شبانی را براه   کو همی گفت ای گزیننده اله

تو کجایی تا شوم من چاکرت   چارقت دوزم کنم شانه سرت

جامه ات شویم شپشهاات کُشم   شیر پیشت آورم ای محتشم

دستکت بوسم بمالم پایکت   وقت خواب آید برویم جایکت

ای فدای تو همه بُزهای من   ای بیادت هی هی و هیهای من

این نمط بیهوده میگفت آن شبان   گفت موسی با کِیست این ای فلان

گفت با آن کس که ما را آفرید   این زمین و چرخ از او آمد پدید

گفت موسی های بس مُدبر شدی   خود مسلمان ناشده کافر شدی

این چه ژاژ ست و چه کفرست و فشار   پنبهٔ اندر دهان خود فشار

گَندِ کفر تو جهان را گَنده کرد   کُفرِ تو دیبای دین را ژنده کرد

چارق و پاتابه لایق مر تراست   آفتابی را چنینها کی رواست

گر نبندی زین سخن تو حلق را   آتشی آید بسوزد خلق را

گر همی دانی که یزدان داور ست   ژاژ و گستاخی ترا چون باورست

دوستیٔ بی خِرَد خود دشمنیست   حق تعالیٰ زین چنین خدمت غنیست

با که می گویی تو این با عمّ و خال   جسم و حاجت در صفات ذوالجلال

شیر او نوشد که در نشو و نَماست   چارق او پوشد که او محتاج پاست

بی ادب گفتن سخن با خاص حقّ   دل بمیراند سیه دارد ورق

لَم یَلِد لَم یُولَد او را لایق است   والد و مولود را او خالق است

هر چه جسم آمد ولادت وصف اوست   هرچه مولودست او زین سوی جُوست

گفت ای موسی دهانم دوختی   وز پشیمانی تو جانم سوختی

جامه را بدرید و آهی کرد تَفت   سر نهاد اندر بیابان و برفت

وحی آمد سوی موسی از خدا   بندهٔ ما را ز ما کردی جدا

تو برای وصل کردن آمدی   یا خود از بهر بریدن آمدی

هر کسی را سیرتی بنهاده ام   هر کسی را اصطلاحی داده ام

در حق او مدح و در حقّ تو ذَم   در حق او شهد و در حقّ تو سَم

ما بری از پاک و ناپاکی همه   از گرانجانی و چالاکی همه

من نکردم امر تا سودی کنم   بلکه تا بر بندگان جودی کنم

هندوان را اصطلاح هند مدح   سندیان را اصطلاح سند مدح

من نگردم پاک از تسبیحشان   پاک هم ایشان شوند و دُر فِشان

ما زبان را ننگریم و قال را   ما درون را بنگریم و حال را

194

ناظر قلبیم اگر خاشع بود   گر چه گفت لفظ ناخاضع رود

زانک دل جُوهر بود گفتن عَرَض   پس طُفیل آمد عَرَض جُوهر غَرَض

چند ازین الفاظ و اضمار و مجاز   سوز خواهم سوز با آن سوز ساز

آتشی از عشق در جان بر فروز   سر بسر فکر و عبارت را بسوز

موسیا آداب دانان دیگرند   سوخته جان و روانان دیگرند

عاشقانرا هر نَفَس سوزید نیست   بر ده ویران خراج و عُشر نیست

گر خطا گوید ورا خاطی مگو   ور بود پُر خون شهیدان را مَشو

خون شهیدان را ز آب اولیترست   این خطا از صد صواب اولیترست

در درون کعبه رسم قِبله نیست   چه غم ار غوّاص را پاچیله نیست

تو ز سرمستان قلاوزی مجو   جامه چاکان را چه فرمایی رُفو

ملّت عشق از همه دینها جداست   عاشقان را ملّت و مذهب خداست

لعل را گر مُهر نَبود باک نیست   عشق در دریای غم غمناک نیست

بعد از آن در سرّ موسی حق نهفت   رازهایی کآن نمی آید بگفت

بر دل موسی سخنها ریختند   دیدن و گفتن بهم آمیختند

چند بیخود گشت و چند آمد بخود   چند پرّید از ازل سوی ابد

بعد از این گر شرح گویم ابلهیست   زانک شرح این ورای آگهیست

ور بگویم عقلها را بر کَنَد   ور نویسم بس قلمها بشکند

چونکه موسی این عتاب ازحق شنید   در بیابان در پی چوپان دوید

بر نشان پای آن سرگشته راند   گَرد از پَرّهٔ بیابان بر فشاند

عاقبت دریافت او را و بدید   گفت مژده ده که دستوری رسید

هیچ ترتیبی و آدابی مجو   هر چه می خواهد دل تنگت بگو

کُفر تو دینست و دینت نور جان   ایمنی و ز تو جهانی در امان

ای مُعاف یَفعَل الله ما یَشا   بی مُحابا رو زبان را برگشا

گفت ای موسی از آن بگذشته ام   من کنون در خون دل آغشته ام

من ز سِدرهٔ مُنتَهی بگذشته ام   صد هزاران ساله زآن سو رفته ام

تازیانه بر زدی اسبم بگشت   گنبدی کرد و ز گردون برگذشت

مَحرم ناسُوت ما لاهُوت باد   آفرین بر دست و بر بازوت باد

حال من اکنون برون از گفتنست   این چه میگویم نه احوال منست

نقش می بینی که در آیینه ایست   نقشِ توست آن نقشِ آن آیینه نیست

دَم که مرد نایی اندر نای کرد   در خورِ نایست نه در خوردِ مرد

هان و هان گر حمد گویی گر سپاس   همچو نافرجامِ آن چوپان شناس

حمدِ تو نسبت بدان گر بهتر است   لیک آن نسبت بحق هم ابتر است

Holy Moses saw a shepherd in the way,
Who was saying, "Oh God, the Selector,
Where are you, so I become your servant?
I sew your clothes and comb your hair,
I wash your attire, kill your lice,
And bring you milk, oh Glorious One.
I kiss your hand, rub your feet,
And at the time of sleep, I sweep your bed.
I sacrifice all of my goats for you,
In my singing and crying I remember you."
The shepherd was saying these frivolous things,
(Holy) Moses said,
"Who is it that you are talking with, oh mister?"
He (the shepherd) said, "With the One who created us,
And formed this Earth and this universe."
Moses said, "You have become very unfortunate,
You haven't become a complete believer,
yet have turned into an infidel.
What is this nonsense and what is this blasphemy and strain?
You should press cotton into your mouth.
The stink of your blasphemy has filled up the world,
Your blasphemy made the silk of religion threadbare.
The head cover and foot cover are worthy of you,
These things are not worthy of the Sun (God).
If you don't shut your throat (mouth) from this chatter,
A fire will come and burn all the people.
If you know that God is the judge,
How can you believe in nonsense and audacity?
The friendship of an unwise man is enmity,
The Grand Almighty is needless of such service.
To whom are you talking – to your uncle and your aunt?
Body and needs are not attributes of the Almighty.
The one who is growing drinks milk,
The one who needs feet wears shoes.
Talking rudely, especially to God (or God's chosen),
Will destroy your heart and make your page black.

Wasn't born and didn't bear a child are descriptions of God,
God is the creator of parent and child.
Whatever has body, birth is its attribute,
Whatever is born is from this side of the stream (world)."
He (the shepherd) said, "Oh, Moses, you sewed my lips,
You burned my soul from remorse."
He tore his clothes and sighed,
And ran in the desert.
A revelation came to Moses from God:
You separated our servant from us.
Did you come for unification,
Or did you come for separation?
I have given everyone different characteristics,
I have given everyone different expressions.
To him it was worship and to you it was a curse,
To him it was honey and to you poison.
We (God) are above all purity and impurity,
Above laziness and diligence.
I did not create to benefit,
But to be merciful toward the people.
The Indians (Hindus) have their own expression of worship,
The people of Sand (Dravidians)
have their own expression of worship.
I do not become pure from their praises,
They become pure and pearl emanating.
We (God) do not look at tongue and talk,
We (God) look at inside (soul) and intention.
We (God) observe if the heart was humble,
Even though the words were arrogant.
Because the heart is the essence,
and the words are accidents;
Accidents are only the means,
the essence is the final cause.
How long will you dwell
on words, nouns, and superficialities?
I (God) want burning (hearts), burning –
endure the burning.
Light a fire in your soul from love,
Burn entirely all thoughts and statements.

197

Oh, Moses the cultured ones are a different kind,
The ones with burned hearts and souls are another kind.
The lovers burn with every breath,
There is no taxation upon a ruined village.
If he speaks in error, do not call him a sinner,
If the martyrs are stained with blood, wash it not away.
The blood is better than water for martyrs,
This error is higher than a hundred pious acts.
Inside of the Ka'ba (Islamic holy site),
there is no need for Ghebleh (direction of prayer),
What concern has a diver for snowshoes?
Do not seek guidance from the drunken ones,
Do not order those with the torn garments to mend.
The nation (religion) of love is distinct from all religions,
God is the nationality and religion of lovers.
If the ruby has no seal (marking) what does it matter?
Love is not sorrowful in the sea of sorrow.
After that, God revealed secrets to Moses,
Secrets that cannot be expressed in words.
They poured words into Moses' heart,
Vision and words combined together.
Sometimes conscious and sometimes unconscious,
He (Moses) soared from the beginning to eternity.
If I describe more than this, it is foolishness,
Because describing this is beyond knowing.
If I say it, it will uproot all wisdom,
And if I write it, it will break many pens.
When Moses heard God's reproof,
He ran into the desert after the shepherd.
He ran after the footprints of the lost one (shepherd),
He raised dust (from running) in the desert.
Finally he reached and saw him,
He (Moses) said, "Rejoice, that a decree was received.
Do not seek any order or method,
Express whatever your tormented heart desires.
Your blasphemy is (true) religion,
and your religion is the light of the soul,
You are saved and the whole world is saved because of you.
Oh, you, who are made secure by God's will,

Go open your mouth without fear."
He said, "Oh, Moses, I have passed beyond that,
I am now soaked in my heart's blood.
I have passed beyond the universe,
I have traveled a hundred thousand years in that direction.
You lashed my horse,
So it jumped beyond the sky.
The Divine World is the secret keeper of our world,
Blessings upon your hand and arm.
My status is beyond explanation,
What I am saying is not my real condition."
You see a reflection in the mirror,
That is your image, not the mirror's image.
The breath that the flutist blows into the flute,
Is worthy of the flute, not the flutist.
Be aware, if you offer thanks or praise,
Know that it is improper like that of the shepherd.
If your praise is better than that,
Still in relation to God it is insignificant.
How often do you say when they took off the veil,
What they were thinking it was not?
The acceptance of your prayer is from God's mercy,

One of the most important morals of this story is that intention is the true essence of prayer, deeds, and actions. In this episode, a learned prophet of God, holy Moses, is confronting an uneducated shepherd and scolding him for his unorthodox and simple manner in which he praises and worships God. However, as God later reveals to holy Moses, to the Almighty the proper words and method are not as important as the shepherd's pure and sincere intention. Therefore, Rumi is explaining that words and appearances do not have as much worth as the intention in front of God. In other words, when you relate to the God of Love, all you need is a pure and sincere heart.

CHAPTER 5

THE HUMAN BODY,

MIND,

SOUL,

POWER,

AND ACTIONS

The Light of God is Man's Original Food

(Mathnavi Book 2, starting from Verse 1084)

قُوت حیوانی مر او را ناسزاست   قُوت اصلی بَشَر نور خداست

که خورد او روز و شب زین آب و گِل   لیک از علّت در این افتاد دل

The original food for Man is the light of God,
The animal food is not worthy of him.
But the heart (soul) fell in this from a disease (cause),
Which eats day and night from this water and clay.

(Mathnavi Book 2, starting from Verse 1081)

روی در قُوت مرض آورده است   قُوت اصلی را فرامش کرده است

قُوتِ علّت را چو چربش کرده است   نُوش را بگذاشته سَم خورده است

گرچه پندارد که آن خود قوت اوست   چون کسی کو از مرضِ گِل دوست داشت

He has forgotten the original food,
He has turned to the diseased food.
He has given up honey and has eaten poison,
He has made the diseased food (as a nourishment) like fat.
As someone who liked (eating) clay from disease,
Though he might suppose that clay is his (natural) food.

(Mathnavi Book 5, Verse 2716)

صد بدن پیشش نَیَرزَد تَرّه توت   عاشقی کز عشق یزدان قُوت خورد

A lover who ate God's love as food,
A hundred bodies to him are not worth
a leaf of a berry plant.

Man's Power

(Mathnavi Book 3, starting from Verse 6)

قوّت جبریل از مطبخ نبود   بود از دیدار خَلّاق وجود

همچنان این قوّت اَبدالِ حقّ   هم ز حقّ دان نه از طعام و ز طَبق

جسمشان را هم ز نورِ اِسرشته‌اند   تا ز روح و از مَلَک بُگذشته‌اند

Gabriel's power was not from the kitchen (food),
It was from seeing the Creator of the Universe.
Similarly, the power of men of God,
You should know, it is from God
and not from the food and tray (carrying the food).
Their bodies also have been created from the light,
So they have transcended the spirit and the angel.

Our Inner Dragon

There is a profound tale in the third book of *Mathnavi* about a man who was a snake charmer. During the winter, he traveled to a snow-covered mountain so he could find some snakes for his show. He found a giant snake (called dragon in the story) that appeared to be dead, but in fact was only frozen from the extreme cold. The snake charmer fastened that giant snake with a rope and brought it toward Baghdad, Iraq. The frozen snake slowly began to revive from the sun and warmer weather in Baghdad. After regaining its strength, it started to move. The snake's movement shocked the people who had gathered to watch the show. The people began to flee, but the snake freed itself from the rope and attacked them like a roaring lion. Many people were killed, including the snake charmer himself. From this story, Rumi draws a wonderful analogy. He explains that our Nafs (sensual desires or carnal soul) is like that frozen giant snake. When the Nafs finds the proper opportunity and environment, it frees itself and becomes the means of destruction. Rumi concludes that we should keep our Nafs, our inner dragon, contained and frozen; otherwise we will be the victims of its revival and subsequent devastation. Why don't I let Rumi, the master storyteller, relate the story in his beautiful poetic language:

(Mathnavi Book 3, starting from Verse 976)

تا بگیرد او بِأَفسونهاش مار	مارگیری رفت سوی کوهسار
گِردِ کوهستان در ایّام برف	او همی‌جُستی یکی ماری شگرف
کی دلش از شکلِ او شد پُر ز بیم	اژدهایی مرده دید آنجا عظیم
مار می جست اژدهایی مرده دید	مارگیر اندر زمستان شدید
زنده بود و او ندیدش نیک نیک	او همی مرده گمان بُردَش ولیک
زنده بود و شکل مرده می نمود	او ز سرماها و برف افسرده بود
می کشید آن مار را با صد زحیر	این سخن پایان ندارد مارگیر
تا نهد هنگامه' در چارسو	تا ببغداد آمد آن هنگامه جُو
غُلغُله در شهر بغداد اوفتاد	بر لب شط مرد هنگامه نهاد

مار گیری اژدها آورده است   بُوالعجب نادر شکاری کرده است

جمع آمد صد صد هزاران خام ریش   صید او گشته چو او از ابلَهیش

منتظر ایشان و هم او منتظر   تا که جمع آیند خلق منتشر

جمع آمد صد صد هزاران ژاژ خا   حلقه کرده پشت پا بر پشت پا

اژدها کز زَمهَریر افسرده بود   زیر صد گونه پلاس و پرده بود

بسته بودش با رسنهای غلیظ   احتیاطی کرده بودش آن حفیظ

در درنگ و انتظار و اتفاق   تافت بر آن مار خورشید عراق

آفتاب گرم سیرش کرد گرم   رفت از اعضای او اخلاط سرد

مرده‌بود و زنده‌گشت او ازشگفت   اژدها بر خویش جنبیدن گرفت

خلق را از جُنبش آن مرده مار   گشتشان آن یک تحیر صد هزار

با تحیر نعره‌ها انگیختند   جملگان از جنبشش بگریختند

بندها‌بگسست‌وبیرون شدچوشیر   اژدهایی زشت غرّان همچو شیر

در هزیمت صد خلایق کُشته شد   از فتاده کُشتگان صد پُشته شد

مارگیرازترس برجا خشتک‌گشت   کی چه آوردم من از کوهسار و دشت

اژدها یک لقمه کرد آن گیج را   سهل باشد خون خوری حجاج را

A snake charmer went to the mountain,
To catch a snake with his expertise.
He was searching for an extraordinary snake,
Around the mountain in the snow time.
He saw a grand dead dragon (giant snake) there,
That his heart became fearful from its shape.
The snake charmer in the harsh winter,
Was seeking a snake and saw a dead dragon;
He suspected it was dead;
It was alive, but he didn't look at it carefully.
The snake was frozen from the cold and snow;
It was alive, but it looked dead.
The snake charmer was carrying that snake,
with a hundred hardships.
Till that adventurer reached Baghdad,
So he could have a show in the main square.
On the bank of the river he started the show,
And in the city of Baghdad the news traveled.
A snake charmer has brought a dragon,
He has done an amazing hunt.

A hundred thousand gathered ignorantly,
They all had become the prey (of the dragon),
like the snake charmer from his foolishness.
They were waiting, so was he,
Till all the people gathered around.
A hundred thousand idle babblers gathered,
They had circled (the dragon), sole against sole.
The dragon that was frozen from the cold,
Was under a hundred kinds of rags and covers.
He had fastened it with thick ropes,
He had taken precautionary measures.
In the meantime,
The sun shined on the dragon.
The sun warmed the dragon sufficiently,
So the cold and frost left its body (organs).
It seemed dead,
but it became alive;
Amazingly the dragon started shaking itself.
From the dead dragon's movement,
People's amazement went
from one to a hundred thousand fold.
From amazement they cried out,
All ran away from its movement.
It broke the ropes and came out like a lion,
An ugly dragon roaring like a lion.
It killed hundreds of people,
Hundreds of bodies piled up on each other.
The snake charmer from fear froze in his place,
(Saying),"What have I brought with me from the mountain?"
The dragon devoured
the bewildered snake charmer in one bite.

Then Rumi continues and makes the most beautiful analogy between the dragon and our Nafs.

(Mathnavi Book 3, starting from Verse 1053)

از غم و بی آلتی افسرده است   نَفسَت اژدرهاست او کی مرده است

هین مکش او را بخورشید عراق   اژدها را دار در برف فراق

206

تا فسرده می بود آن اژدهات لقمهٔ اویی چو او یابد نجات

مات کن او را و ایمن شو ز مات رحم کم‌کن نیست او ز اهل صلات

Your Nafs (carnal soul) is a dragon – how is it dead?
It is depressed from sorrow and lack of means.
Keep the dragon in the snow of separation (from temptation),
Do not take it toward the (warming) sun of Iraq.
So your dragon would remain frozen,
You are its meal if it revives.
Checkmate it and be safe from being checkmated,
Have less mercy (for the dragon),
it is not of the righteous kind.

Rumi talks about our inner struggle with Nafs in the next verses:

(Mathnavi Book 3, Verse 1253)

موسی و فرعون در هستی تُست باید این دو خصم را در خویش جُست

(Holy) Moses and Pharaoh are both in your being,
You must search for these two foes inside yourself.

(Mathnavi Book 3, starting from Verse 971)

لیک اژدرهات محبوس چَهَست آنچه در فرعون بود آن در تو هست

تو بر آن فرعون بر خواهیش بست ای دریغ این جمله احوال تو است

ور ز دیگر آفسان بنمایدت گر ز تو گویند وحشت زایدت

دور می اندازدت سخت این قرین چه خرابت می کند نَفسِ لعین

Whatever was in Pharaoh, is also in you,
But your dragon is imprisoned in a pit.
What a pity all this is in your characteristics,
But you will blame it on Pharaoh.
If they talk about you, you become fearful,
And if (they talk about) others, it seems to you a fable.
The cursed Nafs (carnal soul) will ruin you,
This intimate one (Nafs) throws you far and hard (from God).

207

Good Deeds Never Die

(Mathnavi Book 4, starting from Verse 1201)

ای خُنک آنرا که این مَرکب براند   مُحسنان مُردند و احسانها بماند

وای جانی کو کند مَکر و دَها   ظالمان مُردند و ماند آن ظُلمها

شد ز دنیا ماند ازو فعل نکو   گفت پیغمبر خُنک آنرا که او

نَزد یزدان دین واحسان نیست خُرد   مُرد مُحسن لیک احسانش نمرد

تا نپنداری بمرگ او جان بُبرد   وای آنکو مُرد و عصیانش نمرد

The generous one passed away
and his generosity stayed (behind),
Oh fortunate, he who rides this horse (does this action).
The oppressor died and his injustice stayed (behind),
Alas for a soul who performs trickery and deceit.
The Prophet (holy Mohammad) said,
"Blessed he who left this world,
and left good deeds behind him."
The generous man died, but his generosity did not,
Piety and generosity are not small in front of God.
Alas for he who died and his defiance (to God) did not,
So you should not presume that he was saved by dying.

Happiness is a State of Mind and Thoughts

Rumi discusses the essence of the mind-body relationship in the subsequent verses:

(Mathnavi Book 2, starting from Verse 277)

ای برادر تو همان اندیشه‌ٔ   مابقی تو استخوان و ریشه‌ٔ

گر گلست اندیشه‌ٔ تو گلشنی   ور بور خاری تو هیمهٔ گلخنی

گر گلابی‌بر سر و جیبت زنند   ور تو چون بولی برونت افکنند

Oh my brother, you are all thoughts,
The rest are bones and flesh.
If your thoughts are flowers,
You are a flower garden.
And if your thoughts are shrubs,
You are firewood for burning.
If you are rose water, you are sprinkled on head and bosom,
And if you are urine, you are poured out.

Rumi's above verses are so true. In these present times, we know from the latest medical and psychological research that happiness is really a state of mind. In my next book I have dedicated several sections to a detailed discussion of the most recent research and scientific literature about the relation between human mind and body. The effects of the mind's status are incredible, especially in the areas of age reversal and the production of neurotransmitters and growth hormones and factors. The recent scientific proof about the direct impact of our minds over our bodies is astonishing.

Never Give Up

(Mathnavi Book 1, Verse 3180)

جُنبِشی اندک بکن همچون جنین   تا ببخشندت حواس نور بین

Make a little effort like a fetus,
Then you are granted light-seeing senses.

(Mathnavi Book 1, starting from Verse 1822)

کوشش بیهوده به از خفتگی   دوست دارد یار این آشفتگی

تا دم آخر دمی فارغ مباش   اندرین ره می تراش و می خراش

که عنایت با تو صاحب سِرّ بود   تا دم آخر دمی آخر بود

گوش و چشم شاه جان بر روزن است   هرچ کوشد جان که در مرد و زنست

The Beloved likes this instability,
Fruitless effort is better than sleep.
In this path scratch and carve,
Until the last moment,
do not rest even a moment.
Until the last moment,
there may be a moment,
That the keeper of the secrets (God) has mercy for you.
Whoever is trying, if it is man or woman,
The ear and eye of the King of Life (God)
are at the window (God is listening and watching).

Take Control of Your Own Core Center:
Let Your Actions Be Your Actions,
Not Reactions to Others' Actions

There is an insightful fable in the third book of *Mathnavi* about a horse and its foal drinking water. While they were drinking, people were persistently shouting at them, "Come on! Hey, drink!" The foal became afraid and stopped drinking. The mother asked, "Why did you stop?" The foal stated, "My heart is trembling and jumping from their noises and I am afraid." The mother offered this advice:

(Mathnavi Book 3, starting from Verse 4298)

کار افزایان بُدند اندر زمین   گفت مادر تا جهان بودست ازین

زود کایشان ریش خود برمی‌کَنَند   هین‌توکار خویش‌کن ای‌ارجمند

پیش‌از آن‌کزهجرگردی شاخ شاخ   وقت تنگ و می رود آب فراخ

The mother said, "Since the existence of the world,
There have been meddlers of this kind on the earth.
Oh dear, you do your own work,
Soon they will be pulling their own beards (in regret).
The time is short and the water is flowing rapidly,
(Drink) Before you turn into pieces from separation."

Then the mother continues:

(Mathnavi Book 3, continuing from Verse 4309)

باد می نربایدم ثِقلَم فزود   زآنک هر بادی مرا در می ربود

زآنک نبودشان گرانیٔ قُوی   مر سفیهان را رباید هر هوا

"Because every wind used to sweep me away,
My weight was increased so I would not be taken by the wind.
The fools are swept away by any wind (of temptation),
Since they have no hefty strength."

211

Rumi then teaches us how to apply that valuable lesson to our own lives:

(Mathnavi Book 3, continuing from Verse 4318)

سوی آن وسواس طاعن ننگریم   ما چو آن کُرّه هم آب جُو خوریم

طعنهٔ خلقان همه بادی شُمَر   پی رو پیغمبرانی ره سِپَر

گوش فا بانگ سگان کی کرده اند   آن خداوندان که ره طی کرده اند

We should drink the water from the stream like the foal,
And do not heed those tempting mockers.
If you are a follower of the prophets, tread the way,
Consider people's sarcasm all as wind.
Those Masters who have traveled on the path (far),
When have they ever heeded the dog's barking?

Other meaningful verses in which Rumi further elaborates on this lesson are below:

(Mathnavi Book 1, Verse 2907)

گر شوم مشغول اشکال و جواب   تشنگانرا کی توانم آب داد

If I become involved in answering the criticism,
How can I give water to the thirsty?

(Mathnavi Book 2, starting from Verse 418)

از سگان و عو عو ایشان چه باک   در شب مهتاب مَه را در سِماک

مَه وظیفهٔ خود برخ می گسترد   سگ وظیفه خود بجا می آورد

آب نگذارد صفا بهر خسی   کارک خود می گذارد هر کسی

آبِ صافی می رود بی اضطراب   خس خسانه می رود بروی آب

In a moonlit night, would the moon in the sky,
Have any fear from dogs and their barking?
The dog is performing his duty,

The moon is performing her duty,
by spreading (light from) her countenance.
Everyone performs his own little work,
The water will not lose purity because of a little weed.
The weed floats weedily on the water,
The pure water flows undisturbed.

(Mathnavi Book 6, starting from Verse 12)

گفت از بانگ و علالای سگان   هیچ وا گردد ز راهی کاروان

یا شب مهتاب از غوغای سگ   سُست گردد بَدر را در سیر تگ

مَه فشاند نور و سگ عوعو کند   هرکسی بر خلقت خود می رود

هر کسی را خدمتی داده قضا   در خور آن گوهرش در ابتلا

He said, "From the dog's noise and barking,
Would any caravan stop on its path?
Or in the moonlit night from the dog's barking,
Would the moon falter in its course?"
The moonlight spreads light and the dog barks,
Everyone behaves in accordance with his own essence.
Divine Destiny has given everyone a task,
His essence is appropriate for that task.

What wonderful advice this is for everyone in our turbulent world. If we really look back at our own life, we might see that the majority of our past actions have been reactions to other people's actions, and not our originally intended actions. We easily allow others to take control of our core center and control our actions. As a result, others indirectly manipulate us according to their own agendas. Following our own thoughts requires great self-awareness and self-discipline. Just imagine how much more we could accomplish and how much less we would waste of our time, energy, and life, if others who sought to distract us from our paths could not influence us. In reality, each one of us has to live with the consequences of our own actions. Thus, isn't it wise to act based upon our own thoughts and true interests in the grand journey of life?

Why People Use Drugs and Alcohol

(Mathnavi Book 6, starting from Verse 225)

ننگ خَمر و زَمر بر خود می نهند   تا دمی از هوشیاری وارهند

فکر و ذکر اختیار دوزخ است   جمله دانسته که این هستی فَخ است

یا به مستی یا بشُغل ای مُهتدی   می گریزند از خودی در بی خودی

To flee for a moment from consciousness,
They disgrace themselves with drugs and alcohol.
They all have known that this existence is a trap,
It is volitional thought and remembrance of hell.
They flee from consciousness to unconsciousness,
With drunkenness or occupation, oh the righteous one.

214

CHAPTER 6

FRIENDS

AND

ENEMIES

Spiritual Connection and Attraction

In the second book of *Mathnavi,* Rumi describes the reason for the attraction between people who are spiritually compatible and of the same nature.

(Mathnavi Book 2, starting from Verse 81)

در جهان هر چیز چیزی جذب کرد   گرم گرمی را کشید و سرد سرد

قسم باطل باطلان را می کشند   باقیان از باقیان می‌سرخوشند

ناریان مر ناریان را جاذبند   نوریان مر نوریان را طالبند

خوب خوبی را کند جذب این بدان   طیبات الطیّبین بر وی بخوان

In the world, everything attracts something,
The warm attracts warm and the cold attracts cold.
The worthless kind attracts the worthless,
The worthwhile are rejoiced by the worthwhile.
The people of the fire attract those of the fire,
The people of the light seek those of the light.
The good attracts goodness - know this,
Recite the "Good women for good men"
(a verse from the Koran).

Let Us Appreciate One Other

(Divane Shams, 1535)

که تا ناگه زیکدیگر نمانیم   بیا تا قدر یکدیگر بدانیم

سگی بگذار ما هم مردمانیم   کریمان‌جان فدای دوست‌کردند

غرضها را چرا از دل نرانیم   غرضها تیره دارد دوستی را

چرا مرده پرست و خصم جانیم   گهی‌خوشدل‌شوی ازمن‌که‌میرم

همه عمر از غمت در امتحانیم   چوبعد از مرگ خواهی‌آشتی‌کرد

که درتسلیم ما چون مردگانیم   کنون پندار مردم آشتی کن

رخم رابوسه ده‌کاکنون‌همانیم   چو برگورم بخواهی بوسه دادن

Come and let us appreciate each other,
So suddenly we do not become separated from each other.
The gracious ones sacrificed their lives for friends,
Leave the doggedness - we are also human beings.
Insincerity casts a shadow on friendship,
Why shouldn't we purge our hearts from insincerity?
Will you become happy when I die?
Why are we worshipers of the dead and enemies of the living?
Since you will make peace with me after my death,
My whole life I am being tested by your sorrow.
Now assume that I am dead and make peace with me,
Since in submission I am like the dead ones.
Since you will kiss my grave,
Kiss my face now that I am the same.

This poem conveys a beautiful message. When people pass away from this world and continue to the next one, we usually feel sorrow at their passing even if we have some ill feelings toward them in our hearts. As soon as we hear the news of their so-called death, it seems that our animosity and ill feelings toward them magically fade away. Wouldn't it be logical and rational for us to appreciate them for who and what they are while they are still among us? Even if they have done little things here and there to displease or anger us, we could easily find it in our hearts to forgive them and appreciate being with them while they are physically here on earth. After an individual's physical death, we often regret that we allowed a little disagreement or emotional anger to destroy our relationship with that person and forgot all their good characteristics and qualities. Isn't it much easier and more pleasant for our friends, family members, and ourselves, if we put aside petty disagreements and resentments and make amends before they pass away from this world? In the end, we will miss them and not be able to be with them in their physical forms. Then we will no longer enjoy the privilege of their company and be able to appreciate them for who they are as individuals in this world. Therefore, is it not better to make peace with them right now while they are still here and we have the chance?

Your Enemies Are Your Medicine

The next verses are complex and profound and require some reflection. I will try to shed some light on them later.

(Mathnavi Book 5, starting from Verse 1521)

گر بدانی گنج زر آمد نهان   این جفای خلق با تو در جهان

تا ترا ناچار رو آن سو کنند   خلق را با تو چنین بَد خُو کنند

خصم گردند و عدو و سرکشان   این یقین دان که در آخر جمله شان

The animosity of people toward you in this world,
If you realize, is a hidden gold treasure.
People's tempers are turned against you,
So your face is forcefully turned
toward that direction (God).
Know for certain that all of them at the end,
Become foe, enemy, and rebels.

(Mathnavi Book 6, starting from Verse 2148)

از پی اَلصَبرُ مِفتاحُ الفَرَج   تا کشی خندان و خوش بار حَرَج

گردی اندر نور سُنّتها رسان   چون بسازی با خَسیّ این خَسان

از چنین ماران بسی پیچیده اند   کانبیا رنج خَسان بس دیده اند

Carry the burden smilingly and cheerfully,
Because patience is the key to victory.
When you tolerate the pettiness of these petty ones,
You will reach the light of the prophets' traditions.
The prophets have suffered immensely from the petty ones,
They have often writhed in anguish from such snakes.

(Mathnavi Book 4, starting from Verse 96)

که زحضرت دور و مشغولت کنند   در حقیقت دوستانت دوشمنند

کیمیای نافع و دِلجُوی تُست   در حقیقت هر عدو داروی تُست

In fact, your friends are your enemies,
Who distance you from the Almighty and keep you occupied.
In fact, every enemy is your medicine,
Who is your beneficial alchemy and heart healing.

(Mathnavi Book 3, starting from Verse 4149)

که ترا غمگین کنم غمگین مشو   هر زمان گوید بگوشم بخت نو

تاکت از چشم بدان پنهان کنم   من ترا غمگین وگریان زان کنم

تا بگردد چشم بد از روی تو   تلخ گردانم ز غمها خُوی تو

بنده و افگنده رای منی   نه تو صیّادی و جویای منی

در فراق و جستن من بی کسی   حیله اندیشی که درمن کی رسی

می شنودم دوش آه سرد تو   چاره می جوید پی من درد تو

ره دهم بنمایمت راه گذر   می توانم هم که بی این انتظار

بر سر گنج وصالم پا نهی   تا ازین گرداب دوران وارهی

هست بر اندازه رنج سفر   لیک شیرینی و لذّات مَقَر

ور نه مشکل با برابر جان دهی   هر چه آسان یافتی آسان دهی

My new luck whispers in my ears every moment,
Don't cry if I make you sad.
I make you sad and crying,
So I hide you from the evil eyes.
I make your mood bitter from sorrows,
So the evil eye will turn from your face.
Your pain will seek remedy from Me (God),
Last night I (God) was listening to your cold sigh.
I can without any delay,
Guide you and show you the path.
So you will be saved from the whirlpool of Time,
And you will set foot upon the treasure of My reunion.

220

But the sweetness and the pleasure
of reaching the destination,
It is in accordance with the journey's pain.
Whatever you find easily you lose easily,
Otherwise you keep it dear like your own life.

Since the meaning of some lines may not be very clear at first, let me explain what I believe Rumi is trying to describe here. While you are having some carefree fun with friends, you can easily forget why you are here, what you are doing, and where you are going. While you are enjoying the company of your friends, you lose track and sight of your time, life, journey on earth, and true path. In contrast, when you are disappointed and saddened because of your enemies' actions, your pains and sorrows turn your face back toward the Divine Healer again. You remember the reality of life and reflect upon why you are here and the very reason for your existence. You should not confuse your hedonistic and carefree friends with your true friends, who, according to Rumi, are your mirrors in this life. Rumi explains the mirror metaphor further in the following verses:

(Mathnavi Book 2, starting from Verse 30)

روی او زآلودگی ایمن بود   چونک مؤمن آینهٔ مؤمن بود

در رخ آیینه ای جان دم مَزن   یار آیینه است جان را در حزن

از خس و خاشاک او را پاک دار   یار چشم توست ای مرد شکار

Since the righteous believer is a mirror,
for the righteous believer,
His face is to be protected from corruption.
The friend is a mirror for the soul in sadness,
Oh dear, in front of a mirror do not breathe.
The friend is your eye, oh hunter,
Keep him (like your eyes) clean from sticks and straws.

If we breathe in front of a mirror we make it foggy and cannot see ourselves clearly. While facing the mirror we should just look and observe. A true friend is really like a mirror. Those true friends show you exactly the way you are with all of your strengths and weaknesses. Rumi also reminds us that whatever you easily gain and reach in this life is not as valuable for you as what you obtained with more effort and strife. It is important to remember that the temporary pain and suffering you may endure will not last, but reaching your goal is definitely worth the transitional troubles that you go through in order to achieve it. If you take your eyes away from your goal, it is easy to become focused on obstacles. When we are hurt and heartbroken, we are usually forced to look inwards and get in touch with ourselves. This in turn will focus our attention on our Supreme Creator, and then we can more easily remember the important aspects of our life and our journey in time and space in the universe and beyond.

Your Three Companions in This World

(Mathnavi Book 5, starting from verse 1045)

آن یکی وافی و این دو غدرمند   در زمانه مر تو را سه همرهند

وآن‌سوم وافی‌است وآن‌حُسن‌ُالفعال   آن یکی یاران و دیگر رخت و مال

یار آید لیک آید تا به گور   مال نآید با تو بیرون از قُصور

یار گوید از زبان حال خویش   چون ترا روز ازل آید به پیش

بر سر گورت زمانی ایستم   تا بدین جا بیش همره نیستم

که در آید با تو در قعر لَحَد   فعل تو وافی است زو کن مُلتَحَد

(In your journey)In this world you have three companions:
Two are deceitful and one is loyal.
First are (your) friends,
second are (your) wealth and possessions,
And the third loyal ones are (your) good deeds.
Wealth does not come with you out of palaces,
Friends come, but only as far as your grave.
When your day of departure arrives,
Friend will say from his own sentiments,
"I am only your companion this far,
I will stay at your grave for a (little) while."
Your (good) deeds are loyal,
make them your haven,
Since they will accompany you into the depths of your grave.

224

CHAPTER 7

BE CAREFUL

WHO

YOU FOLLOW

False Assumptions

(Mathnavi Book 5, Verse 871)

تو دل خود را چو دل پنداشتی   جستجوی اهل دل بگذاشتی

Since you falsely assumed
that your own heart is the (real) heart,
Then you abandoned your search for people of the heart.

(Mathnavi Book 1, Verse 2475)

آنچ تو گنجش توهّم می کنی   زآن توهّم گنج را گم می کنی

What you falsely imagine as a treasure,
From that false imagination you lose the real treasure.

Beware of the Charlatans and Imposters

In different books of *Mathnavi*, Rumi warns us about charlatans who call themselves holy and falsely claim that they are spiritual guides and teachers. The subsequent verses are some examples of Rumi's descriptions of those people:

(Mathnavi Book 1, starting from Verse 2276)

پیش او نَنداخت حق یک استخوان   بی نوا از نان و خوان آسمان

نایب حقّم خلیفه زاده ام   او ندا کرده که خوان بنهاده ام

تا خورید از خوان جودم سیر هیچ   الصلا ساده دلان پیچ پیچ

Fortuneless from the sustenance and riches of heaven,
The Almighty has not thrown him even a bone.
He has proclaimed, "I have thrown a feast,
I am deputy of God and a born caliph.
Welcome, tormented and simple-hearted ones (to the feast),
So you can eat your fill of nothing
from my table of generosity."

(Mathnavi Book 1, starting from Verse 2271)

در دلش ظلمت زبانش شعشعی   ظاهر ما چون درون مدعی

دعویش افزون ز شیث و بوالبَشَر   از خدا بویی نه او را نه اثر

تا گمان آید که خود او هست کسی   حرف درویشان بدزدیده بسی

ننگ دارد از درون او یزید   خُرده گیرد در سخن بر بایزید

Our outward appearance,
similar to the inside of the imposter;
Darkness in his heart,
but a shiny tongue.
He has no scent or trace of God,
His claim is greater than that of Seth and Adam.
He has stolen many words of the dervishes,

227

So it may be thought that he is somebody.
In speech, he quibbles with Bayazid (renowned Sufi Sheikh),
But even Yazid (the killer of the Prophet Mohammad's
grandson) would be ashamed of his intention.

(Mathnavi Book 5, starting from Verse 1443)

مِنبَر و مَحفِل بدان افروختند   حرف درویشان بسی آمختند

یا در آخر رحمت آمد ره نمود   یا بجز آن حرفشان روزی نبود

Many words of dervishes they have learned,
They have lit (their) pulpits and sessions with them.
Besides those words they had no other benefit,
Or at the end, Divine mercy came and showed the way.

(Mathnavi Book 1, starting from Verse 2279)

گِردِ آن دَر گشته فردا نارسان   سالها بر وعده فردا کسان

آشکارا گردد از بیش و کمی   دیر باید تا که سِرّ آدمی

عمر طالب رفت آگاهی چه سود   چون که پیدا گشت کاو چیزی نبود

People have gathered at that door for years,
for the promise of tomorrow,
But tomorrow never comes.
It would take long,
Until the human secret is revealed more and less.
When it became clear that he wasn't anything,
The seeker's life (already) was wasted;
what use is (that) awareness?

(Mathnavi Book 1, starting from Verse 2264)

میهمان مُحسِنان باید شدن   بهر این گفتند دانایان به فن

کاو ستاند حاصلت را از خَسی   تو مرید و میهمان آن کسی

نیست چیره چون تُرا چیره کند   نور ندهد مر تُرا تیره کند

چون ورا نوری نبود اندر قران   نور کی یابند از وی دیگران

For this the learned ones have said with wisdom,
"One should become the guest of the generous ones."
You are the disciple and guest of that person,
Who will take your harvest out of his lowliness?
He is not triumphant,
how can he make you triumphant?
He does not emanate light,
he darkens you.
Since he has no light in himself,
How can others acquire light from him?

(Mathnavi Book 6, Verse 2548)

لافِ شیخی در جهان انداخته   خویشتن را بایزیدی ساخته

He has spread the boast of
Sheikhdom (leadership) in the world,
He has represented himself as Bayazid.

(Mathnavi Book 5, Verse 3190)

ای که در معنا ز شب خامش‌تری   گفت خود را چند جویی مشتری

Oh the one, who is more silent than night in meaning,
How long are you searching
for buyers of your (empty) words?

Philosophers Prolong and Complicate Your Path

There is an interesting story in the sixth book of *Mathnavi* about a poor man who was praying to God to relieve him from poverty and make him comfortable. After many prayers he had a dream in which he was told to go to his neighbor's shop, a bookbinder, and look for a piece of paper with a specific color and shape that contained the address of a hidden buried treasure outside of town. The written instructions stated, "Get a bow and arrow and put the arrow in the bow in the direction of Ghebleh (Mecca). Wherever the arrow falls, dig the ground and the treasure is buried there." The poor man followed the instructions and went to that specific place out of town. He put an arrow in the bow, pulled the arrow very hard and dug the ground where the arrow fell, but he didn't find anything. He tried this numerous times with no result. The news spread. When the king of the region heard the news, he summoned the poor man to his court. In the palace, before being tortured, he presented the paper to the king. For more than six months, the king's men under his order followed the same instructions with no result. Finally, the king gave up and returned the directions to the poor man, and told him, "I give up, do whatever you wish to do." Subsequently, the man relentlessly continued praying and begging God to show him the treasure's location. He was engaged in prayer when inspiration came to him and God solved the mystery for him. He was told, "You were told to put an arrow to the bow, but when were you told to pull the bow's string hard? You were not told to draw the bow hard. You were instructed to put the arrow to the bow, and not shoot with your full strength. In your vanity, you raised the bow in the air and tried to elevate the art of archery. This time, put the arrow to the bow and do not draw it. When the arrow falls, dig up the spot and seek the gold and the treasure."

From this simple fable, Rumi draws a profound conclusion about philosophers who act in a similar manner by throwing the arrow of their thoughts too far, making ideas and concepts too complicated and confusing for other people.

230

گو بدو کو راست سوی گنج پشت   فلسفی خود را از اندیشه بکشت

از مراد دل جداتر می شود   گو بدو چنانکه افزون می دود

صید نزدیک و تو دور انداخته   ای کمان و تیرها برساخته

وز چنین گنجست او مهجور تر   هر که دور اندازتر او دورتر

تو فکنده تیر فکرت را بعید   آنچه حقست أقرب از حَبل الوَرید

The philosopher destroyed himself with thoughts,
Tell him that his back is toward the treasure.
Tell him run - the more he runs,
The further he gets from his heart's desire.
You have made bow and arrows ready,
The prey is close and you have thrown your arrow far.
Whoever throws farther, he is farther,
He is farther from such a treasure.
Whatever is right, is closer to you than your vein,
But you have thrown far the arrow of your thoughts.

Rumi's explanation continues further:

هر صباحی سخت تر جُستی کمان   همچو این درویش بهر گنج و کان

بود از گنج و نشان بد بخت تر   هر کمانی کو گرفتی سخت تر

جان نادانان برنج ارزانی است   این مَثَل اندر زمانه جانی است

و آن مراد او را بُده حاضر بجیب   علم تیراندازیش آمد حجاب

گشته رَه رو را چو غول و راه زن   ای بسا علم و ذکاوات و فِطَن

تا ز شرّ فیلسوفی می رهند   بیشر أصحاب جنّت أبلَهند

تا کند رحمت بتو هر دم نزول   خویش را عُریان کُن از فضل و فضول

Similar to this dervish,
that for the sake of the treasure and the (gold) mine,
Every morning he drew the bow more forcefully.
And each time the more forcefully he gripped the bow,
The worst luck he had in finding the treasure and the mark.

This example is of vital importance (to the soul) in the world,
The soul of the ignorant deserves to suffer.
His knowledge of archery became a barrier,
That object of desire was present in his bosom.
Most of the people destined for paradise are simpletons,
Since they escape from the harm of philosophy.
Strip yourself of (useless) knowledge and vanity,
So Divine mercy may descend upon you at every moment.

CHAPTER 8

REPENTENCE,

PRAYER,

AND

THE DAY OF JUSTICE

Repentance

There is a dramatic tale in the fifth book of *Mathnavi* about a man called Nasouh. This man had a feminine face and no one could discern his gender by his face. Because of his temptation, he pretended to be a woman and worked as a shampooer in the women's public bath. As a result, Nasouh was able to see women completely naked, although it was absolutely forbidden and taboo. Many times he had repented to God and seriously considered discontinuing this shameful behavior, but every time, under the force of his temptation, he returned to his job and ignored his repentance. So finally, he went to a spiritual and enlightened man of God and asked him to pray for him.

(Mathnavi Book 5, starting from Verse 2235)

نَفسِ کافر توبه اش را می درید   توبها می کرد و پا در می کشید

گفت ما را در دعایی یاد دار   رفت پیش عارفی آن زشت کار

He was repenting, but turning his back,
The infidel carnal soul was tearing his repentance.
That wrongdoer (Nasouh) went to an Aref (Gnostic),
He said, "Remember me in a prayer."

One day, the king's daughter and her entourage came to the public bath. Since that righteous man had prayed for Nasouh, Divine Destiny wanted to teach him the final and ultimate lesson so he would repent for good. Suddenly it was announced that the princess' pearl was missing and everybody in the bath should be body searched. Nasouh realized that after he took his clothes off they would discover that he was a man and the king would behead him for this audacity and betrayal. Nasouh started to pray, beg, and repent to God and make an oath that if God would free him from this incredible disaster that was coming upon him, he would never break his repentance again. Let's follow the rest of the story in Rumi's own words.

(Mathnavi Book 5, continuing from Verse 2255)

رفت و می‌لرزید او مانند برگ   پیش‌چشم خویش او می‌دید مرگ

توبه‌ها و عهدها بشکسته‌ام   گفت یارب بارها برگشته‌ام

He was seeing death before his eyes,
He went and was shaking like a leaf.
He said, "Oh my Creator, many times I have turned away,
I have broken my vows of penitence and promises."

(Mathnavi Book 5, continuing from Verse 2266)

توبه کردم من ز هَر ناکردنی   گر مرا این بار ستّاری کنی

تا ببندم بهر توبه صد کمر   توبه‌ام بپذیر این بار دگر

پس دگر مَشنو دعا وگفتنم   من اگر این بار تقصیری کنم

"If You cover me this time,
I will repent of every forbidden thing.
Accept my repentance one more time,
So I will dedicate myself a hundred times to repentance.
If this time I commit an offense,
Do not heed my prayer and words."

(Mathnavi Book 5, continuing from Verse 2271)

کان در و دیوار با او گشت جفت   ای خدا و ای خدا چندان بگفت

بانگ آمد از میان جست و جو   در میان یارب و یارب بُد او

گشت بیهوش آن زمان پرّید روح   جمله را جُستیم پیش‌آی ای نصوح

He cried "Oh God, Oh God" so much,
That door and wall joined with him (in worship).
He was in the midst of (calling) "Oh God, Oh God,"
When an announcement came in the middle of the search.
We have searched them all, come forward, oh Nasouh;
He passed out and his soul flew.

235

بعد از آن خوفی هلاک جان بده   مُژدها آمد که اینک گم شُده

بانگ آمد ناگهان که رفت بیم   یافت شد گُم گشته آن دُرّ یتیم

از غریو و نعره و دستک زدن   پُر شده حمّام قَد زالَ الحَزَن

آن نصوح رفته باز آمد بخویش   دید چشمش تابش صد روز پیش

می حلالی خواست از وی هرکسی   بوسه می دادند بر دستش بسی

After that life-destroying fear,
The good news came that the lost pearl is now here.
Suddenly a shout was heard that the danger passed,
That lost pearl was found.
From the noise and shouts and clapping,
the bathhouse was filled,
And sadness had disappeared.
That passed-out Nasouh came around,
His eyes saw the light of a hundred shining days.
Every one was begging his forgiveness,
They were kissing his hand many times.

گفت بُد فضل خدای دادگر   ور نه ز آنچم گفته شد هستم بَتَر

چه حلالی خواست می باید ز من   که منم مجرم تر اهل زَمَن

کس چه می داند ز من جز اندکی   از هزاران جرم و بَد فعلم یکی

من همی دانم و آن ستار من   جرمها و زشتیّ کردار من

اوّل ابلیسی مرا استاد بود   بعد از آن ابلیس پیشم باد بود

حق بدید آن جمله را نادیده کرد   تا نگردم در فضیحت روی زرد

باز رحمت پوستین دوزیم کرد   توبه شیرین چو جان روزیم کرد

هرچه کردم جمله نا کرده گرفت   طاعت ناکرده آورده گرفت

همچو سرو و سوسنم آزاد کرد   همچو بخت و دولتم دلشاد کرد

نام من در نامهٔ پاکان نوشت   دوزخی بودم ببخشیدم بهشت

آه کردم چون رَسَن شد آه من   گشت آویزان رَسَن در چاه من

آن رَسَن بگرفتم و بیرون شدم   شاد و زَفت و فربه و گلگون شدم

در بُن چاهی همی بودم زبون در همه عالم نمی‌گنجم کنون

آفرینها بر تو بادا ای خدا ناگهان کردی مرا از غم جُدا

گر سر هر موی من یابد زبان شکرهای تو نیاید در زبان

He said, "It was the mercy of the just God,
Otherwise I am worse than what was stated.
How can you ask me for forgiveness?
For I am the most sinful of the earth.
What does anyone know about me except very little,
Out of my thousand sins and bad deeds?
I know, and also my concealer (God)
Knows my sins and ugly conduct.
At first the devil was my teacher,
After that the devil was (only) wind in comparison with me.
God saw and ignored them all,
So I would not become yellow-faced in disgrace.
Again God's mercy sewed my clothes (covered my sins),
And (God) granted me a repentance as sweet as life.
Whatever I did, (God) completely undid,
And my unperformed obedience was counted as performed.
(God) freed me like the cypress and lily,
(God) delighted my heart like providence and majesty.
(God) inscribed my name in the book of the righteous,
I deserved Hell; (God) granted me Heaven.
I cried 'Alas', my 'Alas' became like a rope,
The rope was hung into my well.
I grabbed that rope and climbed out,
I became happy, strong, robust, and rosy.
I was miserable at the bottom of a well,
Now, I am not contained in the whole world.
Praises be to You, oh God,
Suddenly you separated me from sorrow.
If the tip of every hair of mine finds a tongue,
Thanking you cannot be expressed."

Prayer Repels Tragedy

(Mathnavi Book 5, starting from Verse 1601)

راه زاری بر دلش بسته کنی   آن که خواهی کز غمش خسته کنی

چون نباشد از تضرّع شافعی   تا فرود آید بلا بی دافعی

جان او را در تضرّع آوری   وآنک خواهی کز بلاش واخری

که بر ایشان آمد آن قهرگران   گفته اندر نُبی کآن اُمّتان

تا بلا زایشان بگشتی باز پس   چون تضرّع می نکردند آن نَفَس

آن گُنَه هاشان عبادت می نمود   لیک دلهاشان چو قاسی گشته بود

آب از چشمش کجا داند دوید   تا نداند خویش را مُجرم عَنید

Whoever You (God) wish to exhaust from sorrow,
You close the path of lamentation to their heart.
So tragedy will descend with no defender (to repel it),
Since there will be no intercessor to plead;
And whomever you wish to save from tragedy,
You lead his soul to plead.
You (God) have stated in the Koran,
That those nations that heavy disasters fell upon.
Since they did not plead at that moment,
That the disaster would turn away from them.
But their hearts had hardened,
Their sins appeared to them as (obedient) prayer.
Until the sinner recognizes himself as disobedient,
How can tears run from his eye?

(Mathnavi Book 5, starting from Verse 1596)

من نتانستم که آرم نا شنود   آب دیده پیش تو با قدر بود

من نتانستم حُقوق آن گذاشت   آه و زاری پیش تو بس قدر داشت

من چگونه گشتمی استیزه گر   پیش تو بس قدر دارد چشم تر

بنده را که در نماز آ و بزار   دعوت زاری است روزی پنج بار

238

The tears from the eyes were precious to You,
I could not pretend not to hear.
Moaning and lamentation were precious to You,
I could not ignore their rights.
The wet eyes have great value to You,
How can I become rebellious?
There is an invitation to lamentation five times a day,
Calling God's servant to come to prayer and lamentation.

The Day Of Justice

(Mathnavi Book 3, starting from Verse 2148)

بر مثال راست خیز رَستخیز   ایستاده پیش یزدان اشک ریز

اندر این مُهلت که دادم من ترا   حقّ همی گوید چه آوردی مرا

قُوت و قوّت در چه فانی کرده   عمر خود را در چه پایان برده

پنج حس را در کجا پالوده   گوهر دیده کجا فرسوده

خرج کردی چه خریدی تو ز فرش   چشم و گوش و هوش و گوهرهای عرش

من ببخشیدم ز خود آن کی شدند   دست و پا دادمت چون بیل و کلند

صد هزاران آید از حضرت چنین   همچنین پیغامهای دَرد گین

دادمت سرمایه هین ینمای سود   نعمتت دادم بگو شُکرت چه بود

Standing in front of God and shedding tears,
Like rising on the Day of Justice.
God is saying, "What have you brought for Me,
During the time that I granted you?
How have you spent your life?
How have you spent your wealth and strength?
Where have you worn out the light of your eyes?
Where have you dispersed your five senses?
What have you bought,
From the expenditure of your eyes, ears, intelligence,
and the celestial jewels?
I gave you hand and foot like mattock and shovel,
I granted them, how could they exist by themselves?
In this way, a hundred thousand painful messages,
Come from the Almighty.
I granted you bounty,
tell me what were your thanks;
I gave you capital,
show me the profit."

(Mathnavi Book 5, starting from Verse 2211)

هم ز خود هرمجرمی رسوا شود   روز محشر هر نهان پیدا شود

بر فساد او بپیش مُستعان   دست و پا بدهد گواهی با بیان

لب بگوید من چنین پرسیده‌ام   دست گوید من چنین دزدیده‌ام

فرج گوید من بکردستم زنی   پای گوید من شدستم تا مِنی

گوش گوید چیده‌ام سُوء الکلام   چشم گوید کرده‌ام غمزهٔ حرام

On the Day of Justice every hidden thing becomes visible,
From his own, every guilty (person) is known.
Hands and feet will utter testimony,
To his sins in front of the Creator.
Hand will say, "I have stolen this way,"
Lip will say, "I have asked this way."
Foot will say, "I have gone to these (desired) places,"
Sexual organ will say, "I have committed adultery."
Eye will say, "I have flirted sinfully,"
Ear will say, "I have listened to bad words."

241

242

CHAPTER 9

THE MAGIC

OF

LOVE

عشق بوی مشک دارد زان سبب پیدا شود
مشک را کی چاره باشد از چنین رسوا شدن

Love has the scent of musk,
For this it is recognized,
Musk has no option but to be recognized.

باز فرو ریخت عشق از در و دیوار من   باز ببرید بند اشتر کین دار من
باردگر شیر عشق پنجه خونین گشاد   تشنه خون گشت بازاین دل سگسار من
باز سر ماه شد نوبت دیوانگیست   آه که سودی نداشت دانش بسیار من
بار دگر فتنه زاد جمره دیگر فتاد   خواب مرا بست باز دلبر بیدار من
صبر مرا خواب برد عقل مرا آب برد   کار مرا یار برد تا چه شود کار من
سلسله عاشقان با تو بگویم که چیست   آنکه مسلسل شود طره دلدار من
خیز دگربار خیز خیز که شد رستخیز   مایه صد رستخیز شور دگر بار من

گر ز خزان گلستان چون دل عاشق بسوخت
نک رخ آن گلستان گلشن و گلزار من

باغ جهان سوخته باغ دل افروخته   سوخته اسرار باغ ساخته اسرار من
نوبت عشرت رسید ای تن محبوس من   خلعت صحت رسید ای دل بیمار من
پیر خرابات هین از جهت شکر این   رو گرو می بنه خرقه و دستار من

خرقه و دستار چیست این نه ز دون همتیست
جان و جهان جرعه ایست از شه خمار من

داد سخن دادمی سوسن آزادمی   لیک ز غیرت گرفت دل ره گفتار من
شکر که آن ماه را هر طرفی مشتریست   نیست ز دلال گفت رونق بازار من

Once again,
love poured from my doors and walls,

244

Once again,
my revengeful camel (of my desire) was cut loose.
Once again,
the lion of love opened its bloody paws,
Once again,
my dogged heart became thirsty for blood.
Once again,
it is that time of the month – the time for madness,
Alas, that all of my knowledge bore no benefit.
Once again,
a new plot was born,
another spark was thrown,
Once again,
my wakeful beloved took my sleep away.
Once again,
my patience fell asleep and my wisdom drifted away,
Once again,
my beloved took my desires away;
I wonder what happened to my desires!
I want to tell you about the chain of lovers,
Each one is a link of my beloved's chain of hair.
Rise,
once again,
rise, rise,
it became the Day of Rising,
My new desire is the cause of hundreds of days of rising.
Even the garden, like the lover's heart,
was scorched from autumn,
The image of that scorched garden
is my rose garden and flower garden.
The garden of the world is burned,
and the garden of my heart is lit,
The burned secret of the garden,
has made the essence of my secrecy.
It is the time for joy, oh my caged body (soul),
Oh my sick heart,
the news of the cure has come.
Oh seer, for this thankfulness,
Go and pawn my robe and shawl for a jug of wine.

What are robe and shawl?
Isn't this from your low aspiration?
The life and world are drops from my enlightened king.
I am bragging about this,
I am a wild lily,
But my heart sealed my lips from passion.
Thank God that beauty has seekers everywhere,
My eminence is not from the broker's advertisement.

Rumi extols love in the succeeding verses in *Mathnavi*:

(Mathnavi Book 1, starting from Verse 23)

شادباش ای‌عشق خوش‌سودای‌ما   ای طبیب جمله علتهای ما

ای دوای نَخوت و ناموس ما   ای تو افلاطون و جالینوس ما

جسم خاک از عشق بر افلاک شد   کوه در رقص آمد و چالاک شد

عشق جان طور آمد عاشقا   طور مست و خَرّ موسی صاعِقا

Be happy, oh our well desired love,
The healer of all our ills.
Oh, the medicine for our pride and arrogance,
Oh (love), you are our Plato and Galen.
Through love, the earthly body soared to the skies,
Mountains began to dance and became agile.
Oh lover, love inspired Mt. Sinai,
Mt. Sinai became drunken and Moses fell in a faint.

(Mathnavi Book 1, starting from Verse 1793)

باغ سبز عشق کو بی مُنتهاست   جز غم و شادی در او بس میوهاست

عاشقی زین هر دو حالت برترست   بی بهار و بی خزان سبز و تَرست

In the green garden of love which has no boundary,
There are countless fruits besides sorrow and joy.
Love is above these two feelings,
The garden of love is fresh and green
without any spring or autumn.

اندرو هفتاد و دو دیوانگی   با دو عالم عشق را بیگانگی

جان سلطانان‌جان درحسرتش   سخت پنهانست و پیدا حیرتش

تَختِ شاهان‌تَخته بَندی‌پیش‌او   غیر هفتاد و دو ملّت کیش او

بندگی بند و خداوندی صُداع   مطرب‌عشق این‌زند وقت‌سماع

در شکسته عقل را آنجا قَدم   پس چه‌باشد عشق دریای عدم

Love is a stranger to both worlds,
In love there are seventy-two states of madness.
Love is hidden and its amazement is apparent,
The soul of the sultan of souls is envious.
Love's religion is separate from the seventy-two nations,
In front of love, the king's throne is (just) a piece of wood.
At the time of Samaa (dance) the singer of love plays,
"Servitude is the chain and lordship is the pain."
What is love? The ocean of nothingness,
There, intellect is like a broken foot.

عشق از اوّل چرا خونی بود   تا گریزد آنک بیرونی بود

Why is love bloody from the beginning?
So the ones who are not worthy of it, will flee from it.

دست مزد و خدمت اُجرَت هم اوست   عاشقان را شادمانی و غم اوست

عشق نَبوَد هرزه سودایی بُوَد   غیر معشوق ار تماشایی بُوَد

هرچه جز معشوق باقی جمله سوخت   عشق‌آن‌شعله‌ست‌کوچون برفروخت

شاد باش ای عشق شرکت سوز زفت   ماند الا الله باقی جمله رفت

God is lovers' joy and sorrow,
God is also their wages and service fees.

If there is any spectacle except the Beloved,
It's not love, it's a false desire.
Love is a flame that, when it flares,
Will burn everything except the Beloved.
God remained and everything else departed;
Hail oh love, the mighty burner of all partnerships.

(Mathnavi Book 5, starting from Verse 2184)

ترس موئی نیست اندر پیش عشق   جمله قربانند اندر کیش عشق
عشق وَصف ایزد است اما که خوف   وصف بنده مبتلای فرج و جوف
زاهد با ترس می تازد به پا   عاشقان پران تر از برق و هوا
کی رسند این خایفان برگرد عشق   کآسمان را فرش سازد درد عشق

Fear is not even a hair in front of love,
Everything is expendable in the path of love.
Love is the description of the Almighty,
But fear is the description of the servant (man)
afflicted by lust and emptiness.
The fearful devout runs on foot,
The lovers leap faster than lightning and wind.
How would the fearful even catch the dust of love?
The passion of love makes the sky its carpet.

(Mathnavi Book 5, Verse 3276)

پیر عشق تُست نه ریش سفید   دستگیر صد هزاران نا امید

Love is your Pir (guide), not the (man with) white beard,
Love lends a hand to a hundred thousand of hopeless ones.

(Mathnavi Book 5, Verse 3230)

پوزبند وسوسه عشق است و بس   ور نه کی وسواس را بستست کس

Love alone is the muzzle of your temptation,
Otherwise, who else could have chained the temptations?

248

(Mathnavi Book 2, Verse 1763)

آتشی از عشق در جان بر فروز   سر بسر فکر و عبارت را بسوز

Light a fire in your soul from love,
Burn entirely all thoughts and statements.

(Mathnavi Book 5, Verse 3241)

حیرتی آید ز عشق آن نطق را   زهره نَبُوَد که کند او ماجرا

An amazement appears from love's eloquence,
No one dares to even tell the story.

(Mathnavi Book 5, starting from Verse 2731)

در نگنجد عشق در گفت و شنید   عشق دریاییست قعرش ناپدید

قطره‌های بحر را نتوان شمرد   هفت دریا پیش آن بحراست خرد

عشق جوشد بحر را مانند دیگ   عشق ساید کوه را مانند ریگ

عشق بشکافد فلک را صد شکاف   عشق لرزاند زمین را از گزاف

با مُحمّد بود عشق پاک جُفت   بهر عشق او را خدا لَولاک گفت

منتهی در عشق چون او بود فرد   پس مر او را زانبیا تخصیص کرد

گر نبودی بهر عشق پاک را   کی وجودی دادمی افلاک را

من بدآن افراشتم چرخ سنی   تا غُلو عشق را فهمی کنی

خاک را من خوار کردم یکسری   تا ز خواری عاشقان بویی بری

خاک را دادیم سبزی و نوی   تا ز تبدیل فقیر آگه شوی

با تو گویند این جبال راسیات   وصف حال عاشقان اندر ثبات

Love cannot be contained in talking and hearing,
Love is an ocean with no bottom in sight.
The drops in the ocean cannot be counted,
The seven seas are miniscule in comparison
with that ocean (love).
Love boils the ocean like a kettle,

Love crumbles the mountain into pebbles.
Love explodes a hundred cracks in the sky,
Love shakes the Earth by its might.
The pure love was Mohammad's mate,
For the sake of love God said, "If it was not for you."
Since he was love's ultimate goal,
Therefore God distinguished him from other prophets.
If it wasn't for pure love,
When would I (God) have created the universe?
I (God) created the universe,
So you may comprehend the glory of love.
I totally demeaned the soil,
So you could discover the lovers' humility.
We gave the Earth greenness and freshness,
So you would become aware
of the transformation of the dervish (lover).
These standing mountains will tell you,
The story of the lovers in steadfastness.

(Mathnavi Book 5, Verse 3854)

گر نبودی عشق بفسردی جهان   دور گردونها ز موج عشق دان

The spinning of galaxies is a wave of love,
Were it not for love, the world would perish.

(Mathnavi Book 5, starting from Verse 2189)

صد قیامت بگذرد و آن نا تمام   شرح عشق ارمن بگویم بردوام

حَد کجا آنجا که وصف ایزَدَست   زآنکه تاریخ قیامت را حَدَست

از فراز عرش تا تَحتَ الثَّری   عشق را پانصد پَرست و هرپَری

If I describe love continuously,
A hundred Rising Days will pass,
and I am still unfinished.
Because the history of the Day of Rising is finite,

Where is the boundary when you are describing God?
Love has five hundred feathers and each feather
Reaches from heaven to eternity.

(Mathnavi Book 1, starting from Verse 112)

هر چه گویم عشق را شرح و بیان   چون به عشق آیم خجل باشم از آن

گر چه تفسیر زبان روشن گرست   لیک عشق بی زبان روشن ترست

چون قلم اندر نوشتن می شتافت   چون بعشق آمد قلم برخود شکافت

عقل در شرحش چو خَر در گِل بخفت

شرح عشق و عاشقی هم عشق گفت

Whatever explanation I say about love,
When I come to love, I am ashamed of my explanation.
Even though the tongue's commentary sheds some light,
Love without commentary is clearer.
The pen in its haste of writing,
When it came to love, broke from love's glory.
In explaining love,
intellect was caught like a donkey in the mud,
Only love could express the story of lovers and the beloved.

(Divane Shams, 636)

در این عشق چو مردید همه روح پذیرید   بمیرید بمیرید در این عشق بمیرید

کز این خاک بر آیید سماوات بگیرید   بمیرید بمیرید و زاین مرگ مترسید

که این نفس چو بنداست و شما همچو اسیرید   بمیرید بمیرید و زین نفس ببرید

چو زندان بشکستید همه شاه و امیرید   یکی تیشه بگیرید پی حفره زندان

بر شاه چو مردید همه شاه و شهیرید   بمیرید بمیرید بپیش شه زیبا

چو زین ابر برآیید همه بدر منیرید   بمیرید بمیرید و زین ابر برآیید

خموشید خموشید خموشی دم مرگست

هم از زندگیست اینک که خاموش نفیرید

251

Die, die in this love,
When you die in this love,
then you all become alive.
Die and die,
do not fear this death,
When you leave this earth,
you soar to the skies.
Die and die,
leave this sensual desire (Nafs),
This sensual desire is a chain and you are the prisoner.
Take an axe to (break) this prison hole,
When you break the prison,
you are all kings and sovereign.
Die and die,
in front of the beautiful King (God),
When you die before the King (God),
you are all kings and renowned.
Die and die,
rise from this cloud,
When you rise from this cloud,
you are all radiant full moons.
You are silent, you are silent,
silence is the moment of death,
It is from living that you are now silent.

(Mathnavi, Book 6, starting from Verse 902)

عشق قهار است و من مقهور عشق   چون شکرشیرین شدم از شور عشق
برگ کاهم پیش تو ای تند باد   من چه دانم که کجا خواهم فتاد
او همی گرداندم برگرد سر   نه به زیر آرام دارم نه زبر
گربه در انبانم اندر دست عشق   یک دمی بالا و یک دم پست عشق
عاشقان در سیل تند افتاده اند   بر قضای عشق دل بنهاده اند
با قضا هرکو قراری می نهد   ریشخند سبلت خود می‌کند

Love is the subduer,
and I am subdued by love,
From love's passion,
I became sweet like sugar.

Oh, fierce wind (of love),
in front of you I am only a straw,
What do I know,
where I will fall?
It (love) is spinning me around its head,
I have no serenity above or below.
In love's hand I am a cat caught in a sack,
From love, one moment up, one moment down.
The lovers have fallen in a severe flood,
They have put their hearts into love's destiny.
Whoever makes a covenant with destiny,
He is mocking his own moustache (himself).

(Mathnavi Book 6, Verse 3647)

دیو اگر عاشق شود هم گوی برد   جبرئیلی گشت و آن دیوی بمرد

Even if the devil falls in love, he will win,
He will become like Gabriel and his evilness will die.

Finally, in *Mathnavi*, Rumi again proclaims the real magic of love:

(Mathnavi, Mohammad T. Marefat Edition, Book 2, Page 138)

از محبّت تلخها شیرین شود   از محبّت مسّها زرّین شود
از محبّت دُردها صافی شود   از محبّت دردها شافی شود
از محبّت مرده زنده می کنند   از محبّت شاه بنده می‌کنند
از محبّت خارها گُل می شود   وز محبّت سرکه‌ها مُل می‌شود
از محبّت دار تختی می شود   وز محبّت بار بختی می شود
از محبّت سِجن گلشن می شود   وز محبّت خانه روشن می شود
از محبّت خار سوسن می شود   بی محبّت موم آهن می شود
از محبّت نار نوری می شود   وز محبّت دیو حوری می شود
از محبّت سنگ روغن می‌شود   بی محبّت روضه گلخن می شود
از محبّت حزن شادی می‌شود   وز محبّت غول هادی می شود
از محبّت نیش نوشی می‌شود   وز محبّت شیر موشی می شود

253

از محبّت سقم صحّت می‌شود   وز محبّت قهر رحمت می‌شود

از محبّت مرده زنده می‌شود   وز محبّت شاه بنده می‌شود

From love, bitter becomes sweet,
From love, copper becomes gold.
From love, dregs become clear,
From love, pains become a healer.
From love, they revive the dead,
From love, they transform king to servant.
From love, thorns become flowers,
From love, vinegar becomes wine.
From love, gallows become throne,
From love, misery becomes luck.
From love, prison becomes rose garden,
From love, house becomes lit.
From love, thorn becomes lily,
Without love, wax becomes iron.
From love, fire becomes light,
From love, devil becomes angel.
From love, stone becomes oil,
Without love, garden becomes furnace.
From love, sorrow becomes joy,
From love, monsters become guides,
From love, sting becomes pleasure.
From love, lion becomes mouse.
From love, sickness becomes health,
From love, fury becomes mercy,
From love, dead becomes alive,
From love, king becomes servant.

In my next book, which should be published very soon, God willing, I have dedicated an entire section to the effect of love on the human body, mind, and spirit. In that book, I discuss some of the latest research in the fields of medicine and psychology to show the effect of love on human mental, physical, and emotional health. These studies once again verify the ingeniousness of Rumi and the importance of his emphasis on the positive effect of love on human mental, physical, and spiritual well-being.

CHAPTER 10

THE

TRUE PATH

The True Occupation

(Mathnavi Book 6, Verse 586, 587)

بهر کار او ز هر کاری بُرید   کار او دارد که حق را شد مُرید

تا شب ترحال بازی می کنند   دیگران چون کودکان این روز چند

He, who became God's follower, has the (real) occupation,
For God's work, he left every other work.
The others, like children, these few days,
Play until the night of departure (from the world).

We Are Nothing Without God's Grace

(Mathnavi Book 1, Verses 1878, 1879)

بی عنایات خدا هیچیم و هیچ   این همه گفتیم لیک اندر بَسیچ

گر مَلَک باشد سیاهستش ورق   بی عنایات حق و خاصّان حق

We said all these words, but in conclusion,
Without God's grace we are nothing, nothing.
Without God's grace and God's chosen ones,
Angel though man be, his page (of deeds) is black.

How true it is. Without God's grace and mercy we are really nothing. In fact, as Rumi has explained, the creation of the whole universe and all the creatures within it is God's expression of love and generosity. If it were not for God's love and kindness, we would not even exist. Without God's protection, we could easily be extinguished by a comet or an asteroid, as millions of them pass our Earth continually.

It was mentioned earlier that Albert Einstein stated that God does not play dice with the universe. This is another indication that the grand architecture of the cosmos is so perfectly designed that nothing is left to chance or random events. The incredible knowledge and ability that have been necessary to create our glorious universe are truly mind-boggling. If you think for a moment about the grandeur of the creation, you will realize what a spectacular feat has occurred at the beginning and still continues to occur. How amazing it is that the universe was created out of almost a nothing point (singularity) and has expanded to become this astonishing structure, which is still expanding and may contract to become that nothing again! It is impossible to even imagine the intelligence, ingenuity, and creative power which designed something so magnificent. We of the human race have only just begun to unlock the amazing mysteries which have been set forth in the creation of our grand universe.

257

In reality, we are small beings in a tiny planet in a majestic and boundless cosmos. In comparison with the Supreme Power we are really insignificant. We are not even able to envision the inconceivable power of the Supreme Master Creator who has created such an infinite universe. Yet we possess a soul that comes from the Almighty. Similar to small drops of water that join the ocean and then become the immense ocean themselves, we can also join with the Infinite Source and become infinite ourselves. Therefore, we should take advantage of every moment in our lives to remain thankful and connected to the Divine Source of Love and express our gratitude through our good thoughts, words, and actions. In this way we will gather more strength and energy for what lies beyond the present moment as we travel the infinite path of our majestic journey toward eternity.

ACKNOWLEDGMENTS

I would like to thank Dr. Firoozeh Naini for her continual support and great dedication to this book. Her invaluable assistance in typing and proofreading, and especially her continual enthusiasm and commitment helped me to continue writing and translating the most beautiful poetry of the master and servant of love, Rumi. Her appreciation and understanding of Rumi's work and poetry was a wonderful source of encouragement for me to push myself to finish this book as soon as possible.

I would also like to thank Dr. Parsa for his wonderful painting. Only a person who has attained a high level of understanding of Rumi's love and teachings could create such an inspired work of art. I could not imagine a better image for the cover of this book.

I would also like to thank all of the people who inflicted upon me the pain and agony which forced me to seek relief through Rumi's most beautiful poetry, insight, and guidance. Without that pain, I might not have been able to appreciate Rumi's teachings and wisdom deep in my heart and soul. As Rumi himself has explained, those people have been truly a beneficial alchemy and medicine for my spiritual growth and enlightenment despite their painful and unjust acts.

BOOK COVER PAINTING

Life works in amazing ways. Wherever I have lived, I have always searched for, or been drawn to, the people of light and love. Thus, I have been very fortunate to meet highly enlightened and spiritually evolved people along my path. The story behind the cover of this book is an example of one such encounter. One day, I suddenly telephoned someone whom I met in the mid-1980s, while I was teaching at the University of Hawaii. In our conversation, he mentioned a gentleman by the name of Dr. Parsa. He told me that Dr. Parsa is very much in love with Rumi's spiritual teachings and poetry. I asked him for Dr. Parsa's telephone number or e-mail, but he replied that he did not have them at hand. I immediately felt an urge to contact Dr. Parsa to at least have the pleasure of conversing with him on the telephone and sharing some of Rumi's thoughts and poetry with him. Thanks to the invaluable tool of the Internet, he was easily found, so I called and left a message on his answering machine. To my pleasant surprise, a very short time later, Dr. Parsa returned my call. From the moment I heard his voice, I felt very much spiritually in tune with him. In fact, after that initial conversation, we have spoken on the telephone for hours, reciting exquisite and insightful poetry to each other. I learned, through our conversations, that he is a very talented artist. He also sent me a book from a friend of his which contained one of his paintings which was directly related to Rumi. One day, as I was meditating, an incredible idea came to me about the cover for my book. The image was Rumi doing his wonderful Samaa in the midst of the universe, while all the galaxies are turning with him. Immediately, a thought came to me that I should talk to Dr. Parsa and tell him about my vision. At first, I was a little hesitant since I knew that he is a very busy plastic surgeon and university professor and he might not have the time to complete such a formidable task. However, I felt a strong impulse to tell him about my thought and let him decide if he wished to paint this magnificent image. Of course, I realized at the time that only an exceptional artist who possessed a special love and connection with Rumi would be able to do this image justice.

When I called Dr. Parsa and told him about my vision, he became so enthusiastic and excited, that it was evident that he indeed is a real lover of Rumi's poetry. Later on, I learned from Dr. Parsa that, from the time I spoke to him, he dedicated his entire free time to create this amazing painting that captures Rumi's euphoria and ecstasy during his Samaa. When he sent me a photograph of the painting, I was fascinated by his grasp of Rumi's exultation and spiritual ecstasy. The colors were so vivid and beautiful, that the more I looked at the painting, the fonder I became of that magnificent artistic piece. At this point, I cannot imagine any other cover for this book. I would like to thank him from the bottom of my heart for his spiritual love, dedication, and hard work. Dr. Parsa mentioned to me several times that Rumi's wonderful spiritual power and force guided his hand, fingers, eyes, and every part of his being as he painted this tribute to Rumi.

Excerpts from Dr. Parsa's Letter
Explaining the Painting

October 4, 2001

Dear Professor Naini,

I immensely enjoyed talking with you on the phone this past Saturday. As you had requested, I am sending you a translation of my thoughts on the paintings of Rumi. I am certain that you can do a much better job on this. However, this is my humble attempt.

I have tried to illustrate and symbolize Love that is the foundation of existence by the swirling motions of many constellations and nebulas. Rumi said in one of his poems: "All particles and all celestial bodies and constellations in motion are moved by the force of love. If such a creative force did not exist, there could be no existence."

The whirling of the constellations with their infinite beauty and harmony point to the infinite beauty and harmony of the whole existence. The stars that are scattered over the entire canvas suggest musical notes and the fascinating celestial music that is created by the movement of the universe.

For Rumi, beauty, love, and music have always coexisted. The majesty of creation with all its wondrous beauty and indescribable celestial music is symbolically reflected in Rumi's heart, in the form of a whirling constellation. The facial expressions of Rumi are drawn with the thought of reflecting love and compassion for all human beings. A Rumi whose purpose is to free the souls of all lovers from their bondage from the mundane daily existence. The doves that fly around him represent the souls of lovers that have been attracted to Rumi and to his universal message. In one poem, he says: "I have built a home within my heart for the soul doves. Come to me. Flap your wings and come to me, O soul doves, whoever you are because I have put together innumerable towers outreaching to the heavens

262

for you to perch on. For how should the dove, nourished, as it is by the beloved's hand, fly to any other place? With fluttering hearts, the lovers approach the beloved, summoned by the beloved's calls and throng with flapping wings around him. The doves that have dwelt on the Friend's roof have reached the highest spiritual peak that can be imagined in this world."

In another poem he sings: "The doves of the soul belong to the vast expanses of heavenly gardens. Do not imprison these doves in the body's cage forever."

And, in another poem he writes: "My poems and my thoughts take their source in the ocean of love so that all humans can discover the Truth and find the water of life that awakens them from their illusions and sleep."

In this painting, Rumi's left hand is reaching into the realm of Truth and Love, that lies above and beyond anything that the human mind can describe in images or words. Rumi's right hand is stretched toward our planet, offering the gift of Love to the entire mankind. I hope that I may have, at least partially, succeeded in showing this gift of Love to the eyes of the heart as clearly as the forms and colors are visible to our external sensory eyes.

I hope that the above translation, from the original Persian although not very literal, will satisfy you. Please feel free to edit or modify in whichever way you wish to. I send you my very best wishes.

Very sincerely,

فریدون پارسا

Fereydoun Parsa, M.D.
Professor of Plastic Surgery
Chief of Plastic Surgery Division
University of Hawaii
John A. Burns School of Medicine

هاواﺉ ١٧ دسامبر ٢٠٠١

هشت عزیز و سرور محترم و دعاگذار گرامی استاد نامجوی

کمال تصور و معنی زمینی محبت دوست ... کورت از دل حافظ پر زحمت رحمت ...

از محبت تلفنی پریشم روز گذشته بسیار لذت بردم و با نظر به رفقا استاد بشری کرشته درباره تابوی

نقاشی اسمی هندو و ترکی و ولایتیان مینویسم بخونه امیدان در چنین شعری نافص میباشد و

استیجاح به حست و قدرت قلم و بلاغت بیان و کار استاد محترم کار دارد تا کریزا به وجه

شایسته تری شرح داده و مانع توهین به مقام پر شکوه مولانا

جلال الدین محمد شبوی پیلو نه ملک است سلیمان نورانی چنین عارفی

عظمتش در صحیح ما با حساب و قلبی نمی کنجه در

روی یک تابوی محدود کاورد؟ حستی و تشویق ای استاد عزیز و محترم د

عشقی ا به مذاو روزگار دارم و الهامی که از از سوی رفقا و عاشقان

مذاو روزگار به این حقیر رسیده به دستور من از آن جرات را بخشیه ام قلم و

هرگت گیرم و در نگاها با ارشک پنجم دایکه و این تعبلو راگ کهی کانم

در سطح تا بود و شش کسه ام که با موجهای پیا ... که هیکشان بوجود آورده ...از

شا لوده دهستی با امواج عشق ات بروز هریم

دور گر دو خدا ز امواج عشق دا گر بودی عشق نبودی جها

چرخش حرکت شان با زیبائی و موزونیت و هارمونیش ارشان به زیبائی موزو

و هارمونی طلیه موجودات در این جهان میلند و پر الهنه ... گستارگا

ارشان به نوقهای موسیقی و اهنگهای دل انگیزی می کنند

که از آفرینش و امواج عشق بدانند هسته و شکلی نیست

از ازل زیبائی و عشق بهم بهم بافته مولد ... بهم آهنگ سرودائی داشته انز

بانک در جشنهای چراغ ارت این انتقی می سرایند بی طنبور و به حلق

ما همه اجزای کرم نوحه ایم در هشت آن لحظه ها بشنوده ایم

در چه بر ما لحت ایک و گل شلی یا دمان آمده از رگ ها چیریم

پس غذای عاشقی آمد سماع که درو با شده خیال اجتماع

265

سعی کرده‌ام که عبدل و شکوه در آفرینش ... با تمام زیبائی و امواج

... عاشقانه در کشف یک همراهی موسیقی غیر قابل وصف ... در ... مبارک خداوندگار

باز تاب یافتم و همچنین درک می‌کنم که این مربوب ظاهراً نمایان ... در باطن دنیا

شکوه و ... عظمتی دارد که در دل و جان جهان ... در چرخش هستند

و مقدار ... گفته‌ام که او ت که با ... جهان خودیش دردو ... جبر برچرخ ... گشته

باده در جوشش گدای ... چرخ در گردش از همین است ...

یا و ... و یک ... بسم ... از عشق برآمد ک شد

خوبه در رقص ... آمد و پیدا ک شد

... که از عشق و مهربان و محبت به نهایت خدا و ... با در

... راه باز تاب به ... میل و شده ... به گفتار ... نشین و ... بخش ...

مرغ جان مردمان سال از ... این دنیای ... بیرون آورده و از آزاد ...

مثنوی آزادی یافته مانند پرندها ... دیوانه‌ای هستند که در اطراف

دل و اندیشه مولانا در چرخش هستند :

266

جون مرغ خانه ای در دام اجبو تر های مبا خدا

بتیر ای مرغ جان آزین سوی اختدای حصیله دلام

یاد ور میتک دمی مولانای سراییت

مرغ باغ ملکوتم نیم از عالم خاک

چند روزی قفسی ساخته اند از بدن

این در یای پی پنبا ای عشق یا عالم ملکوتس در مکان لامکان جای دارو

شده اوزگار با دکت چپ مبا کش از که باغ و بوستان اند او از

ای دنیای بقا و حقیقت مبا ودا د میوه های عشق و معرفت را گرفته و

توسط دکت این در خذذ که به قلوب و دل نقتکا حق و حقیقت

عنایت مخصه و حبا خدا ای زنده و برای تحف تازه و تلفت احدا ده میا

امید وار م ا ان استاد عزیز و محترم این چند سطر ا بپسند فر

نجمت فیر د راه خدمت عرض سلام وارم

یاهو

فریدون نادری

267

ENDNOTES

[1]All of the reference materials I have utilized regarding Rumi are printed in Farsi with the exception of *The Mathnawi of Jalaluddin Rumi* by Reynold A. Nicholson (London: Messrs Luzac & Co. Ltd, 1972) and *The Triumphal Sun* by Annemarie Schimmel (Albany, NY: State University of New York Press, 1993).

[2] For more information on the Big Bang theory, readers are encouraged to read Stephen Hawking's works, including *A Brief History of Time* (New York: Bantam Doubleday Dell, 1988) and *The Universe in a Nutshell* (Toronto: Bantam Doubleday Dell, 2001).

[3] The following books, articles, and websites are recommended for more information on the mysteries of the universe:

The Elegant Universe: Superstrings, Hidden Dimensions, and the Quest for the Ultimate Theory by Brian Greene (New York: W.W. Norton & Company, 1999).

"Dark Matter in the Universe," by Vera Rubin in *Scientific American*, March, 1998.

"The Cosmic Far Ultraviolet Background," by Stuart Bowyer in *Annual Review of Astronomy and Astrophysics,* 1991 (29: 59-88).

www.nasa.gov   www.sciencemag.org
www.sciam.com   www.newscientist.com
www.spacetoday.net   www.spaceflightnow.com
www.hubble.stsci.edu   www.pbs.org/wgbh/nova/universe

[4] To find out more about Dr. Ahrens' work, it is suggested to read *Meteorology Today : An Introduction to Weather, Climate, and the Environment* (New York: Brooks/Cole Pub Co, 1999).

[5] To find out more about Dr. Chopra's work, it is suggested to read *Quantum Healing* (New York: Bantam Books, 1989), *How to Know God* (New York: Harmony Books, 2000), and Dr. Chopra's others books.

INDEX

A

Adam, 129, 146, 147, 148, 172, 173, 178, 227
Aflaaki, 4, 5, 45
Ahrens, C. Donald, 149, 268
Akhiyan, 17, 42, 72, 82
Alast, 146
Ala-uddin, Rumi's younger son 12, 17, 23, 33, 44, 46, 79
angel, 95, 148, 154, 181, 203, 254
Armavi, Ali Turk, 72
Aseman, 12, 13
Asia, 3, 11
Asrar Nameh, 11
Attar, 11, 72
attraction, 26, 50, 52, 123, 216

B

Baghdad, 11, 204, 205
Baha-e-Valad, Rumi's father, 10, 11, 12, 14, 15, 27, 65
Baha-uddin, see Sultan-Valad
Balkh, 10, 11, 12, 13, 22, 57
Bayazid, 20, 22, 65, 228, 229
Bibi Alavi, Rumi's mother, 12
Bible, 143
Borhan-uddin Mohaghegh, see Termezi
Bowyer, Stuart, 130, 268

C

caravanserai, 50
certainties of life, 137
Cheleh, 14
Chopra, Deepak, 151, 268
continual renewal, 149
contradiction, 141, 142
creation, 80, 86, 92, 114, 115, 116, 118, 120, 141, 143, 156, 257, 262
cycle of life, 154, 157

D

Damascus, 15, 34, 39, 42, 44, 53, 54, 55, 61
dark matter, 131, 132
Day of Justice, Day of Rising, 107, 160, 133, 240, 245
death, 13, 16, 18, 46, 72, 79, 154, 157, 160, 180, 181, 217, 235, 252
dependency, 21, 26, 32, 33, 44, 45, 57, 60, 184
devil, 172, 173, 237, 253, 254
Divane Motonab-bee, 27
Divine Destiny, 92, 168, 173, 180, 187, 190, 213, 234
dream, 69, 76, 91, 98, 147, 160, 169, 230

E

Earth's rotation, 124, 125
Ebne Arabi, 15, 50
Einstein, Albert, 115, 257
Elahee Naameh, 72
electromagnetic, 86, 113, 130,
    133, 157
enemies, 219
eyesight, 130

F

Fanaa, 57
Farsi, 1, 2, 10, 54, 117, 268
Fatwa, 15, 17, 18, 57
Fawayed Valad, 27
fear, 87, 92, 99, 100, 103, 104,
    199, 206, 212, 236, 248, 252
Fihi-Ma-Fihi, 83
Foroozanfar, 1, 5, 39
frequency, frequencies, 4, 105,
    113, 120, 130, 131, 133, 134,
    138, 165
friends, 11, 40, 63, 72, 171, 217,
    218, 220, 221, 222, 223

G

galaxy, galaxies, 95, 113, 115,
    117, 122, 126, 131, 132, 140,
    147, 150, 178, 196, 250, 260
Gharatay, 29
Ghazal, 34, 35, 36, 37, 38, 39,
    40, 56, 60, 65, 74
Ghazzali, Iman, 4, 88
Gheysariyeh, 14, 16

Gohar Khatoon, Rumi's first wife,
    12, 18
gravity, 4, 113, 115, 122, 123
Greene, Brian, 132, 268

H

Hadith, 10, 17
Hafez, 51, 74
Hajj, 11
Hamedan, 11
Hanafi, 15, 83
Hawking, Steven, 115, 268
heaven, 27, 54, 79, 86, 100, 103,
    105, 146, 147, 148, 173, 178,
    227, 251
Hegelian Dialectic, 140, 142
Hejri Ghamari, Islamic lunar
    calendar, 5
Hosam-uddin, 18, 33, 72, 74, 75,
    76, 78, 79, 80, 81, 82
Hubble, Edwin, 122

I

infrared, 130, 131
inward knowledge, *Elme Hal*, 22
Iqbal, Afzal, 5, 56

J

Jaami, 5, 10, 45
Jafari, Mohammed Taghi, 5
Jesus, 188, 189, 190
journey of life, journey of
    discovery, 2, 3, 11, 16, 23, 26,
    57, 173, 213

K

Kad Kani, Shafiee, 5, 102, 106, 155
Kamal-uddin Ebne Ala-uddin, 15
Kera Khatoon, Rumi's second wife, 18, 33
Keykhosro, 16
Keymia, 18, 44, 45, 47
Khaaghaani, 72
Khalifeh, 61, 63, 65, 72, 78, 80, 83
Khaneghah, 17, 82
Khayyam, 11
Khergheh, 50
Khorasan, 10, 12, 25, 50, 178
Konya, 10, 12, 13, 14, 16, 17, 18, 25, 29, 32, 39, 42, 44, 45, 50, 51, 52, 53, 54, 55, 57, 63, 72, 82
Koran, 10, 15, 17, 73, 146, 148, 216, 238

L

Larandeh, 11, 12

M

Maghalote Shams, 28
Majalese-Sab-eh, 18
Malamatiyyan, 51
Mantegho-tair, 72
Mecca, 5, 11, 230
meditation, 3, 15, 70, 120
mind-body relationship, 209
mirror, 61, 107, 134, 145, 199, 221

Mohammad, 5, 10, 11, 17, 20, 22, 50, 70, 80, 118, 208, 228, 250
Molana, 10, 14, 15, 34, 42, 60
Moreed, 33, 82, 83
Moses, 64, 112, 145, 192, 193, 196, 197, 198, 199, 207, 246
Motonab-bee, 27
Mufti, 15
music, 2, 11, 26, 27, 33, 55, 57, 68, 146, 148, 262
mysteries, 35, 105, 112, 120, 132, 257, 268

N

Nafs, 16, 204, 206, 207, 252
Namaz, 64, 70, 72
negative forces, 140
Newton, Isaac, 122, 123
Neyshaboor, 11, 12
Nezaami, 72
Nicholson, Reynold A., 1, 5, 74, 268
nuclear, 4, 113, 116, 122, 126

O

opposite, opposites, 87, 136, 140, 141, 142, 143, 144, 145
outward knowledge, *Elme Ghal*, 22

P

Parvaaneh, Moin-uddin, 82
path of love, 3, 5, 16, 23, 26, 57, 64, 74, 86, 100, 101, 171, 248

peace, 2, 10, 17, 20, 33, 44, 45,
    50, 53, 64, 70, 72, 80, 86, 99,
    105, 113, 118, 140, 141, 142,
    175, 176, 187, 188, 217, 218
Pir, 248
prayer, 46, 60, 64, 70, 82, 182,
    188, 189, 198, 199, 230, 234,
    235, 238, 239
prophets, 14, 18, 20, 73, 192,
    212, 219, 250

Q

quantum physics, 4, 142

R

radiation, 130
reality, 22, 24, 25, 26, 87, 92,
    105, 113, 115, 120, 131, 137,
    138, 180, 181, 213, 221, 258
rebeck, 58, 69, 147
reed, 27, 74, 75, 170
regret, 45, 168, 169, 170, 173,
    211, 218
religion, 10, 15, 21, 63, 83, 88,
    104, 105, 141, 146, 164, 196,
    198, 247
repentance, 45, 65, 234, 235,
    237
Resurrection, 142, 146, 148, 172,
    176
reunion, 51, 52, 53, 54, 69, 86,
    103, 146, 147, 156, 220
reunion, 142
Rezgh, 186, 187
rhythm, 2, 3, 74

Rubaiyat, 46, 73, 89
Rubin, Vera, 131, 268

S

Salah-uddin, 18, 23, 33, 60, 61,
    63, 64, 65, 72, 73, 80, 82
Salek, 16
Saljoghi, 12
Samaa, 2, 26, 27, 28, 32, 33, 35,
    39, 44, 51, 53, 54, 55, 57, 60,
    61, 63, 68, 69, 70, 72, 73, 79,
    80, 97, 99, 147, 247, 260
Sanaie, 72, 74
Schimmel, Annemarie, 5, 46, 268
science, 4, 112, 113, 137, 164,
    257
seclusion, 23, 25, 27, 28, 33, 39,
    53, 58, 179
secret eye, 112, 113
senses, 112, 113, 115, 128, 129,
    130, 133, 134, 210, 240
sensual desire, see Nafs
Shams
    and Rumi's students, 28, 29, 30
    early days, 50
    first disappearance, 32, 33, 34
    meeting with Rumi, 20, 21, 23
    returning to Rumi, 42, 43
    second disappearance, 45, 46, 47,
        53, 54
    teachings, 51, 52, 57, 88
Sheikh, 16, 17, 18, 20, 23, 27,
    29, 50, 61, 63, 65, 82, 95, 98,
    228
singularity, 115, 257
Solomon, 43, 180, 181

Soroush, Abdul Kareem, 5, 74
spirit, 26, 81, 97, 156, 203, 254
Sufi, 4, 10, 17, 20, 42, 50, 65,
    72, 80, 103, 120, 228
sultan, 10, 11, 13, 16, 70, 247
Sultan-Valad, 12, 17, 23, 33, 39,
    42, 43, 46, 53, 54, 61, 65, 79
sustenance, 183, 184, 185, 186,
    190, 227

T

Tabattol, 57
Tabriz, 25, 29, 35, 38, 50, 52,
    54, 55, 57, 88, 103, 156, 179
Tabrizi, Shams' father, 25, 50
technology, 4, 113, 257
Termezi, 10, 13, 14, 15, 16, 22,
    28, 72
theologian, 4, 15, 16, 18, 22, 50,
    52, 54, 79, 86, 104
theology, 13, 15, 22, 64, 97

U

ultraviolet, 130, 131, 134
universe, 2, 31, 52, 61, 86, 87,
    91, 92, 95, 98, 99, 102, 105,
    107, 112, 114, 115, 116, 117,
    118, 120, 122, 130, 131, 132,
    138, 148, 149, 150, 165, 175,
    176, 187, 189, 199, 222, 250,
    257, 260, 262, 268

V

veil, 22, 26, 27, 70, 77, 78, 134,
    135, 137, 169, 199
vibration, vibrational, 131, 133
vision, 3, 92, 130, 131, 135, 138,
    165, 170, 260

W

WIMP, 132, 133

Z

Zarinkoob, Abdul Hussain, 5
Zekr, 15

ABOUT THE AUTHOR

Dr. Majid M. Naini received his B.S. Degree in Electronics Engineering and his Master's Degree in Computer Science. He has a Ph.D. in Computer and Information Science from the University of Pennsylvania, the birthplace of ENIAC, the first digital computer in the world. For most of the past 24 years Dr. Naini has been a Professor, Program Director, Laboratory Director, Department Chair, and College Dean at eight major universities throughout the world in the fields of Computer Science, Engineering, and Information Technology. Professor Naini is a world traveler who has lived and taught in four different continents.

Professor Naini has been an active researcher and the designer of several state-of-the-art Computer and Information Technology projects with various multi-national corporations. He has obtained numerous grants and contracts from various funding organizations and industries for research and development of high tech products. He has been an invited speaker at over 100 national and international conferences, seminars, workshops, symposiums and talks. He is the author of numerous innovative books and papers in the field of science, technology, mysticism, and spirituality.

For the past 30 years of his life, Dr. Naini has been a student of mysticism, Sufism, poetry, literature, history, and numerous traditions and cultures. Dr. Naini considers "the great Persian mystics (*Aref*) and poets, Rumi, Hafez, Saadi, Attar, Khayyam, Asiri Lahijee, Hatef Esfahani, Abu-Saeid Abul-khair, Mahmoud Shabestari, and others as his spiritual teachers who have taught him about the higher aspects of the human existence and the journey of the soul."

In his books and lectures, Dr. Naini combines the latest scientific findings and discoveries of various scientific disciplines with mysticism and spiritualism, and expresses his

274

findings and thoughts through the astoundingly beautiful poetry of the greatest mystics of all time, such as Rumi.

Dr. Naini conveys the message that "love, is the most magical force in the universe that can quicken the flow of the energy of one's soul. Through love, human beings can soar to the peak of their existence and reach the highest state of ecstasy. After all, love was the reason for the creation of the universe and what it contains." He also explains, "Happiness is a state of mind and love is the healer of all ills." Dr. Naini states, "Universal love surpasses all the boundaries of race, color, nationality, gender, religion, tradition, civilization, history, custom, and culture. As love is universal, so is the truth. Human beings from all different ethnic, cultural, historical, and geographical backgrounds share the same magnificent journey of life."

Dr. Naini presents the poetry in his books and lectures both in the original Persian language (Farsi) and his own English translations from the most accurate Farsi texts.

SEMINARS AND WORKSHOPS

Dr. Majid Naini offers seminars and workshops in English and Persian on various topics including Rumi, Sufism, spirituality, science, and technology.

To get in touch with Dr. Naini, please contact him at:

E-Mails: DrNaini@Naini.Net
              DrNaini@Yahoo.Com

Telephone: 561-272-6102

FAX: 707-788-5024

Website: www.naini.net

Address: Universal Vision and Research
              P.O. Box 7401
              Delray Beach, FL 33482
              U.S.A.